DATE DUE

DEMCO, INC. 38-2931

The
Job-Generation
Controversy

The
Job-Generation
Controversy

The Economic Myth of Small Business

David Hirschberg

M.E. Sharpe
Armonk, New York
London, England

Library of Congress Cataloging-in-Publication Data

Hirschberg, David, 1934–
The job-generation controversy : the economic myth of small business /
David Hirschberg.
p.   cm.
Includes index.
ISBN 0-7656-0490-6 (hc. : alk. paper)
1. Labor supply—United States. 2. Job creation—United States.
3. Small business—United States—Employees. I. Title.
HD5724.H555   1999
331.12′042—dc21   99-27548
CIP

Printed in the United States of America

For Amy, Stacy, and Steve

Thou shalt not have in thy bag divers (various) weights, a great and a small. Thou shalt not have in thine house divers measures, a great and a small. But thou shalt have a perfect and just weight, a perfect and just measure shalt thou have: that thy days may be lengthened in the land which the Lord thy God giveth thee.

—Deuteronomy XXV:13–15

Contents

Acknowledgments

This book began as a memorandum that summarized my analysis of the job-generation process by firm size.

I shared that memorandum and subsequent drafts with several economists and statisticians whose help was invaluable. They include Seymour Ehrlich, a friend for over forty years. His passing in April 1998 has saddened many of us who will miss his keen intellect and good humor.

Several others who aided in this effort should be noted: Samuel Ehrenhalt, former New York regional director of the Bureau of Labor Statistics; Professor William Dickens, formerly with the Council of Economic Advisors and now with the Brookings Institution; Thomas Jabine, my former boss at the Social Security Administration, who continues to make important contributions to the statistical community and the

Washington Statistical Society; and Norman Frumkin, a colleague at the Bureau of Economic Analysis and author of *A Guide To Economic Indicators* and *Tracking America's Economy*.

At critical times, they provided a sense of direction when it was most needed. They asked questions that led to insightful results. Early on, they forced me to focus on things that were important, and all were generous with their time, making valuable suggestions that helped clarify complex data presentation issues. Their encouragement will always be appreciated.

Jim Lynch, vice president for Business Development, Social and Scientific Systems, and Barbara M. White made important editorial comments.

Finally, my wife, Ronnie, who has been a tower of strength for me for thirty-eight years, spent many hours reviewing this manuscript and made many valuable suggestions. Without her love and support, I could not have written this book.

The
Job-Generation
Controversy

Chapter 1

Introduction

For the public, jobs are what economic policy is all about. Through their jobs, people obtain the income they need to pay for cars and washing machines, food and clothing, visits to the doctor, and a college education for their children. A job often provides a sense of identity, even a sense of self-worth. Losing a job can be devastating.

A nation's economy depends on its ability to create jobs.

For years, politicians have been saying that small business creates all the jobs—or at least the vast majority. This claim is a powerful propaganda weapon, and both politicians and the small business lobby know it.

The U.S. Small Business Administration (SBA) has long made grossly distorted claims about the role of small business in job generation. Under the guise of helping small business, the agency has promoted and popularized this falsehood. This book will show the true role of small business in job creation.

The SBA's Office of Advocacy was created in the 1970s. Its purpose is to lobby for small business. Since then, the claim "small business creates all the new jobs" has become the mantra of both political parties. Cited as "fact," this claim is used to justify preferential treatment for small business. Yet this "fact" is nothing but a hoax perpetrated by the SBA and the National Federation of Independent Business (NFIB). It is a hoax that many elected and appointed officials in both parties have bought into. And economists who know the falsity of this claim have been effectively silenced by the SBA.

In 1996, during the vice-presidential debate, Jack Kemp argued with evangelical fervor for a small business capital-gains cut to grow the economy faster. "How about the small businessmen and women of America that create 91 percent of the jobs?" he asked. In more recent speeches, he has railed against those who contradict his argument. Rather than present the data, he asserts that small business is innovative, is creative, and makes an important economic contribution.

Writing in newspapers, magazines, and journals, nonpartisan economists and authors have pointed out the statistical fallacy underlying the SBA's assertions. Until 1994, however, no reliable comprehensive national data were available to assess the SBA's claims.

Upon my request, in the spring of 1994 the U.S. Bureau of the Census provided employment data for firms in the entire private nonfarm economy for the 1982-91 period. In addition, for the first time, special tabulations were prepared for 1989-91, showing changes in employment by size of firm. The matrix classifies firms by their employment size in 1989 and in

1991. This allows for the examination of firms by employment size category to determine how firms of different size
contribute to the job-generation process.

Analysis of the Census Bureau data exposes the statistical
fallacy on which the SBA's claims are based. The data reveal
a tremendously dynamic economy. It is precisely this dyna-
mism that the SBA wrongly identifies as job generation. The
Census Bureau data reveal that if you and your spouse both
work but for different firms, the chances are three in four that
at least one of you has worked for a firm that has laid off
workers in the last two years.

What the SBA calls job generation is really an aspect of
employment volatility—the combined effect of job creation
and job destruction.

The Census Bureau data tell a story different from the one
promoted by the SBA. No matter what business size measure
is used—less than 20 employees, less than 100 employees, or
less than 500 employees—it is clear that small business not
only did not create all the jobs but, in fact, destroyed jobs.

The focus here is on Census Bureau data for the 1989-91
period, although they are now several years old. Nevertheless,
the results are comparable with data for the 1982-87 period
and the 1991-93 period. For the latter period, the full detailed
data are not available to me in analyzable form because of
confidentiality constraints. Census Bureau data for the three
periods can be obtained from the SBA. The Census Bureau
has informed me that, at the SBA's request, it is not producing
current job-generation data for recent periods in the necessary
matrix format, so that employment change by size class can
no longer be analyzed for more current periods.

How has the SBA been able to fool the public? By using a

statistical trick. If you went to the track, bet $10 on each of eight races, and collected only $65, obviously you lost $15. It would not be telling the truth to say that you won $65. Yet for almost two decades, the SBA has ignored the small business employment losses and reported only its employment gains.

This job-generation controversy exists, in large part, because the SBA has used the "regression fallacy" to promote the job-generation hoax. To understand the regression fallacy, just look at our race track bettor. The SBA counts its winnings but not its losses. Thus, it can claim that 91 percent of the jobs are created by small business.

And no one looks at the statistics. No one asks the SBA a few simple questions: How many jobs were actually created and destroyed during the period? How many jobs were actually created and destroyed by businesses that were small in both 1989 and 1991? By businesses that were large in 1989 and 1991? By businesses that were small and then became large, and by businesses that were large and then became small?

The SBA has written press releases, articles, and reports, arguing that small businesses create virtually all the jobs. Yet it never answers these simple questions.

I will.

Using Census Bureau statistics, I will show that large business created all the jobs. Furthermore, the employment gains of large business more than offset the employment losses of small business. The 91 percent claim is pure smoke and mirrors.

What is at stake in this job-generation claim is no less than the economic well-being of millions of Americans. Whether the issue is minimum-wage legislation, taxes, environmental regulations, or mandated employer health insurance benefits, the small business job-generation argument is made. And unfortunately, the result hurts millions of Americans.

If you think I exaggerate the impact of the small business job-generation argument, examine the minimum-wage debate in the 1996 Congressional Record. Virtually every congressional opponent of raising the minimum wage argued that to do so would hurt small businesses, and that they create all the jobs. What the record does not show is the passion and verve expressed by each opponent of raising the minimum wage, while the mantra, "Small business creates all the jobs," is repeated.

This book not only exposes the SBA's phoney claims. It also explains what is at stake for our society as the rich get richer and as the poor lose their health insurance, lose their work-site safety protections, pay disproportionately higher taxes, incur ever greater debt to educate their children, and have less job security than before.

This book

- explains why 15,000 of the largest firms employ half of all workers and reveals who the true job creators are;
- provides data demonstrating that you are four times more likely to be laid off if you work for a small firm than if you work for a large one;
- reveals why millions of workers are losing their health insurance every year;
- explains how the most powerful Washington lobby, the NFIB, exploits the SBA's phoney numbers;
- explains why the Council of Economic Advisors failed to tell the American people the truth about the job-generation process;
- provides a "new" theory of business size that explains

how our competitive system creates the distribution of
employment by business size;

- explains that firm formation and firm discontinuance
rates are significantly higher than previously reported by
the SBA, which used private data resources to estimate
firm births and deaths, and therefore understates the
volatility of small business employment.

The SBA has been successful at keeping relevant Census
Bureau information out of the hands of economists and statisticians. Furthermore, the SBA has used federal resources to
mount a campaign of disinformation about the role of small
business in generating jobs. The SBA's counting rules are
based on a statistical fallacy. They are part of a deliberate
effort to deceive the public on this vital, emotional issue. The
argument that small business creates all the jobs is a powerful
weapon in the political arsenal of the SBA and NFIB.

Organization of This Book

In Chapter 2, I discuss the politics of the job-generation issue
and review the job-generation controversy. The statistical
agencies of the federal government operate under a cover of
secrecy, arguing that they are duty bound to protect confidentiality. Therefore, these job-generation employment claims have
never before been examined for the total nonfarm workforce.

In Chapter 3, I explain the "regression fallacy." No responsible economist has used the methodology of the SBA's
Office of Advocacy to estimate job generation. And many
economists have called attention to the SBA's misleading interpretation of the statistics. Even Milton Friedman, a pro-
business economist, has written about the SBA's hoax, but his

insightful analysis has been ignored.

In Chapter 4, I analyze the newly available Census Bureau firm and employment data. This is the first in-depth analysis of these data. Like the SBA, I define "small firms" as those with less than 500 employees. Yet my findings in Chapter 4 hold for "small" firms of whatever size. By compensating for the jobs lost by small business, the Census Bureau data show that large business creates all the jobs. That finding holds for small-firm cutoffs at 5, 20, 50, and 100 employees.

The data demonstrate that the changes in employment created by small firms that become large and large firms that become small essentially cancel each other out. I find an amazing symmetry in the number of firms increasing and decreasing their employment. This same symmetry also exists in the flow of workers between size groups. It is this crucial phenomenon that the SBA ignores in its estimates of job generation.

In Chapter 5, I explain the nation's highly skewed firm employment size distribution. I show how the industrial organization gaming model can be applied. The gaming model not only predicts the future distribution of jobs by firm size, but also explains how our current employment size distribution developed. I show not only why the distribution of employment by firm size is likely to remain unchanged—as it has for more than fifty years—but why this very skewed employment distribution is the same in all democratic industrial countries.

Technical appendices are provided for economists and statisticians who may be interested in additional detail and analysis. They include Census Bureau, industry job-generation data for all major industry divisions, computer instructions for generating similar quantitative data, and other material for interested students.

Chapter 2

The Job-Generation Myth
A Political Issue

Nothing causes a worker more anxiety, apprehension, and concern than losing a job. A person who is laid off from work goes through enormous emotional and economic upheaval. For one thing, the person faces the double whammy of being unemployed and not having an income. If, as is often the case, there is a recession going on, the prospects of getting another job may be poor. And the loss of a job often means the loss of health insurance as well.

Because of the unavailability of high-paying jobs and the increasing time it takes laid-off workers to find new jobs—particularly comparable jobs—the focus of economic policy has been on maximizing employment opportunities.

For the economy as a whole, there is little question about

how to define job creation. Job creation means the change in the number of jobs in the total economy. Current monthly data are available to track these trends.

When job creation is looked at by business size, however, the issue becomes less clear. For example, jobs can be counted by establishment, firm, legal entity, or enterprise size. (An enterprise may have many establishments.) In addition, the time lags involved in the preparation of statistical files and in data availability by business employment size mean that here the economist is not analyzing what is occurring now but what has already occurred. And when job creation is looked at by business size, the application of counting rules becomes more complex because some firms may have merged while others may have divested themselves of various activities.

The analysis of job generation by business size means determining the number of employed workers in small and large businesses and the contribution each group has made to total employment. It is not always clear how to do this. If, for example, a large auto company finds the demand for its product growing, it hires more workers and places more orders with its suppliers, many of which are small. These small firms then hire more workers. Who should get the credit for creating the jobs in these small firms? Such questions cannot be answered simply by examining employment growth in small and large companies over time.

Theoretically, the most efficient firms should grow faster than the less efficient firms. Productivity measures of firms of varying sizes—for firms above a minimal size—have been reported to be flat. Therefore, the question of which type of firm size is more efficient can only be answered empirically.

How The Small Business Administration's Office of Advocacy Contributes to the Myth

Extraordinary claims have been made regarding the job-generation capabilities of small businesses. An SBA Office of Advocacy news release of September 30, 1994, stated, "New data from the U.S. Bureau of the Census show that the nation's smallest firms—with 0-4 employees—created virtually all the new jobs between 1989 and 1991." The news release continued, "The smallest businesses (0-4 employees) created 2.6 million jobs."

This number could not have been accurate. It was four times the number of jobs created by all firms.

Other statements from the Office of Advocacy in news releases and reports reinforce the proposition that small businesses created the "vast majority" or "over 80 percent of jobs." The implication is that small businesses are the saviors for those seeking jobs. An Advocacy publication, *The White House Conference on Small Business* (April 1994), reported similar findings on small business job generation:

> During the recent recession, it was the small businesses of the nation that rallied, kept going, and added jobs. From 1988 to 1990, all of the net new jobs in the economy were created by small firms. During this period, the performance of the nation's smallest firms (those with fewer than 20 employees) was extraordinary; they created almost 4.1 million new jobs.

These claims are a hoax. The SBA and the small business lobby have been successful in perpetuating these claims because no one had any reliable data to show that small businesses, in fact, were net job destroyers.

"Small business creates nearly all the new jobs," headlined

Washington Technology on December 5, 1996. That article stated: "According to estimates prepared by the NFIB based on data from the SBA, businesses with fewer than 100 employees have created two out of every three jobs, said a spokesman for the Washington-based association."

Earlier, in October 1996, SLATE magazine published my article, "Small-Biz Blarney: What Does It Take to Kill a Bad Number?" (www.slate.com; search on Small-Biz Blarney or on Hirschberg, author). There, I presented a simple table showing that small businesses actually lost jobs, that small businesses were not the job creators, and that the SBA's claims were false. I used the SBA's definition of small—less than 500 employees. I reported for the 1989–91 period and showed that small businesses, those with fewer than 500 workers, lost 192,000 jobs, while large businesses added 802,000 (a statistic that *Washington Technology* also reported). I did not report on data for firms with less than 100 workers.

In response to the December 1996 *Washington Technology* article, I wrote in a letter to the editor that an analysis of the data for the same period clearly indicates that those firms with fewer than 100 workers lost 40,000 jobs, while large businesses added 650,000. The analysis also reveals that a worker is four times more likely to lose a job when working for a small business than when working for a large one. The Census Bureau data that are available directly contradict the SBA's and NFIB's mantra about small business and job creation.

The Myth's History and Some of Its Implications

More is at stake here than an obscure political/statistical debate. The emotion-laden issue of job generation has affected the nation's legislative agenda in health reform, minimum-wage legislation, and the federal regulatory process. The job-generation argument in the hands of these small business advocates is used to impoverish Americans.

How did this myth get started? In *The Job Generation Process* (a 1979 report to the U.S. Department of Commerce, Economic Development Administration), Dr. David Birch made the claim that small businesses created the vast majority (80 percent) of jobs. This claim quickly became a mantra for those advocating preferential treatment of small business. The NFIB and SBA used this mantra to good effect to kill employer-mandated health insurance reform. When NFIB opposed raising the minimum wage, it repeated the mantra, and when it pressed its job-generation argument, it gained major tax concessions.

During the health care reform debate in 1994, those opposed to an employer mandate argued that small businesses are the job generators. If small businesses are forced to raise payroll costs by covering an additional 12 million or so workers, they insisted, jobs will be destroyed. This argument tapped into real fears.

Because nothing was changed, last year, two million more workers and their families were identified as not having health insurance; virtually all were employed by small companies.

A Political Strategy of Deception

Using the same database as David Birch, the Dun and Bradstreet Market Identifier file, the Office of Advocacy began a database project in 1979 to "confirm" Birch's results. In 1993, the SBA inspector general characterized the data as unreliable and recommended that they be replaced by relevant and reliable data from federal agencies. The Office of Advocacy then abandoned the project but continued the mantra.

How can a campaign of disinformation based on a statistical fallacy gain such widespread acceptance, particularly in the age of the Internet? Why have academic papers and newspaper articles that have called attention to this fallacy had no notable effect?

One reason is that the Office of Advocacy and others in the SBA have doggedly perpetuated this hoax. Another is that many in the nation's capital have an interest in hiding the truth.

The argument that "small business creates all the jobs" has a strong political payoff. For example, during the 1996 vice-presidential debate, when Jack Kemp, arguing for a small business capital-gains tax cut, asserted that small business creates 91 percent of all the new jobs, Al Gore did not see it as advantageous to correct him.

In addition, the Office of Advocacy and others making the job-generation claim never made available reliable and comprehensive data on the changing size distribution of firms. The SBA's Office of Advocacy never prepared tables in any systematic way so that employment changes by firm size—including births of new firms, deaths of existing firms, and growth of existing firms—could be measured adequately.

The Office of Advocacy never produced or tabulated or generally made available data in such a way that would allow independent statisticians and economists to study the problem in a statistically unbiased fashion.

Regulatory Reform: Strengthening the
Regulatory Flexibility Act

The job-generation issue has entered the vital arena of regulatory reform. At issue is the Regulatory Flexibility Act (Reg Flex), an arcane feature of the regulatory process. The SBA and NFIB have vigorously promoted legislative changes to subject this act to judicial review. If proposals to "strengthen" this obscure piece of legislation are adopted, the results could be disastrous for the regulatory process and the agencies that oversee that process.

Most citizens do not know what Reg Flex is about. In reading the following explanation, do not be turned off by its seemingly abstruse nature. Remember that what is at stake is clean air, clean water, and a safe work environment.

In 1979, Congress changed the Administrative Procedures Act, which spells out how federal rules and regulations are to be made, including giving public notice, providing time for comment, and letting those affected know what is occurring. Reg Flex imposed new requirements. It required that regulatory agencies report to the Office of Advocacy on how a proposed regulation will affect small businesses and do a "cost-benefit" analysis of its impact on small business. Unfortunately, the data, funds, and knowledge to do such an analysis are not available.

The dirty little secret is that the costs and benefits of cleaner air and water, a safer work environment, and safer cars—all of which have been accomplished by regulation—cannot be readily or reliably measured as the Reg Flex requires. Nor can the regulatory agencies estimate the total cost of such regulation, much less the effect on small business compared with large business. When the regulatory agencies raise questions relating to problems of measurement impact, the Office of Advocacy offers no expertise.

Ours is a complex economy. Predicting the impact of a regulation or of a change in the way business is conducted is imprecise at best. It is still unclear, for example, how the North American Free Trade Act (NAFTA) has affected U.S. companies and their workers, much less how it has affected businesses of various sizes. The unavailability of data is only part of the problem.

The regulatory agencies have never stated the obvious—that they had no way to measure economic impacts on businesses of various sizes. Instead of stating that we cannot predict with any certainty the economic impact on small businesses of removing lead from gasoline or DDT from our arsenal of pesticides, the regulatory agencies have fudged this Reg Flex analysis requirement.

A congressional staffer suggested this analogy to me: A patient consults a doctor for an ailment. After examining the patient, the doctor tells him that he will not recover unless he runs four miles each day. The patient knows he is incapable of running even half a mile. However, he is afraid to tell the doctor. He promises to run the four miles at midnight, but he does not run at all. The doctor sees the patient again, notes no improvement in his condition, and makes his instructions stronger. The patient must not only run the four miles, but he must run them during the day, and a third party must attest to his compliance. This is the dilemma that will face agencies if the legislative "reform" of Reg Flex passes.

This is not to say that there should not be better analyses of regulatory costs and benefits. Such analyses would help us establish priorities and allocate limited resources. However, because of confidentiality concerns, the data needed to do these analyses and make intelligent choices are unavailable to the regulatory agencies and to the Congress.

Furthermore, the proposed mandatory judicial review of the Reg Flex provisions is counterproductive to a rational, effective regulatory process. Once a regulatory issue gets into the federal courts, it may never be settled. The business community generally wants "judicial reform," which would give the courts less of a role in business affairs. Paradoxically, in this instance, the business community wants to see the judiciary embroiled in the regulatory process, a task the courts are ill equipped to handle.

Although the Office of Advocacy is charged by Congress with administering the Reg Flex Act, it cannot even provide Congress with an evaluation of the SBA's basic regular 7(a) guaranteed loan program. The 7(a) loan program is the SBA's main business loan activity. When Congress provided funds to study the 7(a) loan program in 1985, the Office of Advocacy—after spending nearly a million dollars in worthless, unproductive, and meaningless studies—said the evaluation could not be done. The SBA itself has ignored or exempted itself from the Reg Flex provisions. Early in 1995, the SBA changed its regulations as to the maximum loan it would guarantee, raising the amount to $750,000 from $500,000. The SBA cannot evaluate the "economic impact" of this regulatory change, and it never even tried.

I believe that Reg Flex reform is a formula for chaos. Its so-called "business supporters" in the Congress should realize that NAFTA and the General Agreement on Tariffs and Trade (GATT), which were basically reductions in reciprocal tariff rates, could have been delayed interminably in the courts, if this judicial review legislation had been in place. We need to understand what is happening to our economy and the implications of proposed regulatory and economic changes. The courts should have little to do with the issues.

The interplay between politics and the misguided ideology surrounding the Reg Flex issue was apparent in 1993. In order to obtain Senate approval of its nominee to head the SBA, the Clinton administration was forced to endorse the congressional proposal for the judicial review of Reg Flex.

Health Insurance Reform

In 1994, the Congress failed to act on employer-mandated health insurance coverage. It would have benefited mostly poor working Americans—those working in small businesses that provided no health insurance. Medicare and Medicaid, for the most part, cover the older population and those on public assistance. Large businesses cover virtually all their employees. People who are uncovered are all employed by small businesses. Each year since 1994, over one million additional workers, virtually all in small businesses, lost their health insurance coverage. Every year, about two million additional workers and their dependents will continue to lose their health insurance. This trend will continue because the proposed employer mandate was defeated.

The reason for the declining health benefit coverage is easy to understand. As the cost of health insurance goes up, it becomes more burdensome for businesses to provide health insurance for their workers. As additional workers lose their health insurance they, as a last resort, use hospital emergency rooms. This is an expensive form of care. It raises the overall cost borne by those already insured. As rates go higher, fewer employers are able to provide insurance, and additional workers are then left without insurance.

The mantra that "small business creates all the jobs" was used to good effect during the debate. Politically, there are two possible ways to provide health coverage for the entire population. The first is through a single-payer system, such as the Canadians enjoy. There is little support for this revolutionary change. Therefore, the only politically feasible method is to enact an employer mandate.

Because of the current leadership in Congress, there is nothing on the table. During his 1995 testimony on the minimum-wage issue, Labor Secretary Robert Reich indicated that an employer mandate lacked congressional support. Therefore, an increasing number of workers will continue to lose health benefits. The small firms that pay a major portion of their workers' health insurance will be at an economic disadvantage compared with firms that do not cover their workers. All things being equal, firms that provide health insurance will do less well because of higher costs. As those firms that do not provide health insurance expand at the expense of those that do, workers will be denied basic health care.

While workers in companies that provide health insurance may be more productive, have lower rates of turnover, and feel more loyalty than workers in other companies, it is hard to demonstrate to business that these factors offset the higher costs of health insurance.

If the Democrats in Congress in 1994 had understood what was at stake politically, the politics of the last decade of the twentieth century would have been different. Newt Gingrich understood the political importance of the health care debate and made every effort to kill the health reform proposal. The Republican leader knew that if the Democrats passed a significant health care reform package, they would be assured of a majority in Congress for another twenty years.

The Public Record

Small businesses, those with fewer than 500 workers—to use the SBA's definition of small—employed 49 million out of the 93 million workers in the U.S. economy in 1991. Everyone agrees that the small business sector is important to the economy. However, its plea for special treatment should be based on the facts.

It is noteworthy that the plea for less burdensome regulation is generally couched in terms of helping small businesses because they create all the jobs. Congress has exempted small businesses from many of the regulations that it enacted. The Americans with Disabilities Act excludes small firms, as do the Family Leave Act and many of the Occupational Safety and Health Administration (OSHA) rules regarding accident record keeping and the like.

In his 1993 state of the union address, given shortly after taking office, President Clinton stated:

> Because small business has created such a high percentage of all the new jobs in our nation over the last ten or fifteen years, our plan includes the boldest targeted incentives for small business in history. We propose a permanent investment tax credit for the small firms in this country. . . .

In the Republican response that same evening, the House

Minority Leader, Robert Michel, was not going to be outdone:

> We agree with the president that we have to put more people to work, but remember this: 80 to 85 percent of the new jobs in this country are created by small business. So the climate for starting and expanding businesses must be enhanced with tax incentives and deregulation, rather than imposing higher taxes and more government mandates.

Overwhelming numbers of legislators have been victims of this propaganda and misrepresentation. They repeat it unthinkingly. When, at the start of the 1995 Congress, the new Speaker of the House of Representatives, Newt Gingrich, was asked about the SBA's budget, he replied that we cannot cut the SBA because small business creates all the jobs.

More than $1 billion could be cut from the federal budget simply by eliminating the SBA. Are education, job training, and school lunch programs better budget targets?

The SBA's major activity, the 7(a) loan program, guarantees loans made by cooperating banks to small business. It is assumed that there is some kind of market failure and that these guarantees, which help banks, are necessary to promote small business because there is a lack of small business capital. Yet no one has ever demonstrated that there really is any kind of market failure.

The claims that small business is the fountainhead of job creation are not isolated. Fallacious claims about the job-creation powers of small businesses appear with remarkable regularity in speeches by prominent politicians of both parties, by opinion-makers in their newspaper articles, and by statements of the SBA's Office of Advocacy and other SBA officials. In speeches, press releases, annual reports, and background papers, the small business mantra is chanted. Any effort within the federal statistical and economic establishment to counter these erroneous statements encounters sharp hostility.

The Mantra's History

As I mentioned earlier in this chapter, the first "findings" were published by David Birch, a researcher at MIT. He prepared a study, *The Job Generation Process,* in 1979 for the Economic Development Administration of the U.S. Department of Commerce using Dun and Bradstreet's Market Identifier File. By creating a longitudinal data file of establishments, Birch was able to examine their employment growth over time.

Unfortunately, his conclusions rested on a misinterpretation of the data. Washington is a town where every issue is debated ad nauseam. However, Birch's claim that 80 percent of the jobs were generated by small businesses was never subjected to careful statistical scrutiny. No one looked at the data. No one was even given access to the data.

In 1988, Birch seemed to recant. In an article in the *Wall Street Journal,* "The Hyping of Small Business," David Wessel and Buck Brown quoted Birch as arguing that the 80 percent was a silly number and meant almost nothing: "I can change that number at will by changing the starting point or the interval." Later, I will explain why Birch said that. He now concedes that his 80 percent statistic is "misleading and uninteresting."

In that *Wall Street Journal* article, Dun and Bradstreet (D&B) reported that it had not been able to replicate Birch's numbers. It quoted Joseph Duncan, chief economist and statistician for D&B: "I'm troubled that our data is used to say things that we can't."

To its credit, D&B generated a longitudinal database to study the business employment climate and the job-generation process. For analysis purposes, Duncan developed a sample file of a few thousand firms, editing these sample reports with considerable care to create a small business database. The D&B findings are regularly reported, and they cannot verify the SBA's Office of Advocacy's claims.

The lead article in the business section of the June 25, 1995, *Boston Globe* examined the job-generation question. In that article, Birch is quoted as saying that his claim that small businesses create all of the jobs is "dysfunctional" (the *Globe*'s quotation).

To the contrary! Later I will show that the question of employment size distribution and the related issue of job generation tell us a great deal about the nature of our competitive industrial economy.

The SBA's Technical Role

Until the so-called D&B database project was terminated at the recommendation of the SBA's inspector general, the Office of Advocacy spent more than $14 million of its research budget to try to bolster Birch's argument that small businesses generate virtually all the jobs. Using the same D&B data source as Birch, the SBA contracted with several consulting companies to edit D&B's Market Identifier file and prepare special "job-generation" tables.

The SBA's Office of Advocacy's methodology was flawed. Academics who pointed this out were ignored, and pressure was put on those who objected.

Advocacy's handling of the small business database project—in which the D&B data files were a major component—stands as a model of how not to resolve statistical problems in large files. There were internal inconsistencies in the D&B files, as might be expected from a large-scale collection program that was not designed for statistical analysis purposes. Although D&B does an excellent job of maintaining and updating its files, basic problems with the system affecting the statistics were never resolved. More to the point, without extensive fieldwork, there was no way to account for data anomalies.

The Dun and Bradstreet File

There are major drawbacks to using the D&B Market Identifier data for job-generation purposes, and these problems are well known. For multi-establishment companies, there are identified headquarter records' "pointers" identifying their establishments. A pointer is an entry in a computer record that identifies another record. Briefly, there are a large number of records identified as multi-establishment headquarters records, but no establishment records of plants could be matched to them. Conversely, there were a large number of multi-establishment records without a headquarters company.

In addition, the employment statistics were misleading. They did not conform to regularly published Census Bureau and Bureau of Labor Statistics totals. The SBA's detailed industry employment data were not comparable with complete counts obtained from tax records. New firms could not readily be identified, and out-of-business companies could not readily be purged. In addition, the smallest firms that never sought credit were difficult to identify.

Even more devastating findings about the utility of the data set appeared in a 1984 Government Accounting Office (GAO) study of plant closings. Congress was then trying to find out what was happening in the Rust Belt (the northeastern and midwestern states, where heavy industry has declined) and asked the GAO for a report. In making its study, the GAO went to the SBA. The SBA used a D&B sample of firms that either lost a significantly large number of workers in the period 1982-84 or had significant employment in 1982 but were dropped from the 1984 file.

After reviewing the data on the sampled firms, the GAO called a special meeting with Advocacy's economists and statisticians. The GAO prepared a report indicating that of its sample of 2,152 firms reporting either mass layoffs or plant closings, data on only 19 percent were correct. In the remaining 81 percent of the cases, Advocacy's data were incorrect and unusable for statistical purposes. These findings were replicated by the Massachusetts Employment Commission that used 1981-82 D&B data for the same purpose.

These reports were made known to the SBA's inspector general. The inspector general's report of July 1991 (Audit Report No. 1-4-001-277) concluded that the Office of Advocacy's D&B project was a boondoggle, that it was eating up an increasing share of Advocacy's budget, that it did not provide reliable statistics, and that arrangements should be established with the regular government statistical agencies to obtain needed statistics. The July 1991 memo from the assistant inspector general for auditing to the acting chief council for advocacy recommended canceling the D&B project, citing the above arguments, and pointed to an annual savings of more than $1 million. These recommendations were parallel to my own suggestions and were supported by a majority of the Advocacy staff when the inspector general interviewed them privately.

Despite the inspector general's report, Advocacy continued to publish the job-generation data, which were out of touch with the real world. The inspector general's report and the virtually unanimous support of the working staff for terminating the D&B project are never mentioned in any Advocacy document relating to its database efforts.

In the spring of 1993, Erskine Bowles was appointed the SBA administrator. His initial address to the SBA staff was like a breath of fresh air. Unfortunately, the open attitude he expressed did not carry through.

On May 3, 1993, I addressed a memo to Bowles through formal administrative channels on "Job-Generation Data Problems—What the New Administrator Should Be Told." The first paragraph stated: "The new administrator should not be blindsided by the job-generation issue. He should be told directly that there is no reliable statistical evidence to support the proposition that small business is the chief creator of new jobs."

The memo and its attachments—special studies, articles, tabulations, and a paper by a colleague in Advocacy—all documented problems with the D&B data. The attached articles noted the difficulties in the small business sampling frame of the D&B file; the above-mentioned GAO report, which called attention to the quality and reliability of the job-loss data; and comparisons of the D&B data with Census Bureau and Bureau of Labor Statistics data from the 1989 *Statistical Abstract of the United States,* which showed the official government nonfarm employment data to be at variance with Advocacy's tabulations of nonfarm major industry employment from the D&B files.

The Academics Weigh In

My memo to Bowles included copies of two articles, one by Milton Friedman, who had won a Nobel Prize for economics, and one by Jonathan Leonard, an economist at the University of California, Berkeley. Leonard's article was the first academic empirical attack on the job-generation myth. *On the Size Distribution of Employment and Establishments* appeared in 1985 as National Bureau of Economic Research (NBER) Working Paper #1951. Using special business files from state unemployment insurance tax data, Leonard showed that the SBA's methodology was fallacious and flawed and that the distribution of firms by size was unchanged over a period of time. He also reported that other employment measures of size-of-firm data were virtually unchanged over long periods of time. The SBA and NFIB never cited Leonard's findings. The Office of Advocacy did not respond to his research.

Milton Friedman's article, "Do Old Fallacies Ever Die?" appeared in the December 1992 *Journal of Economic Literature.* When I attached this to my memo, I underscored the pertinent paragraph: "For example, 'everyone knows' that job creation comes mainly from small firms. That proposition may be true but the evidence offered for it that I have seen classifies firms by size in the initial year and traces subsequent levels of employment—precisely what Secrist did." (Secrist was trying to show that enterprises were tending to converge in size. Paradoxically, I will show later that the Census Bureau data indicate that there has been no change in the employment size distribution of firms since 1946.) Friedman continued, "I have yet to see what the data show if firms are classified by their terminal size." (Later, when the new Census Bureau data are analyzed, I will show that if firms are classified by their terminal size, then large businesses create twice the number of jobs created by businesses.)

I suspect that Friedman's article was the most widely read economic journal article in the quarter in which it appeared. Most members of the American Economic Association receive the *Journal of Economic Literature* (*JEL*). Although one would expect an article by Friedman to be provocative, insightful, and educational, I was pleasantly surprised by Friedman's specific observations on the job-generation issue.

Finally, I felt I had an ally whose Nobel-laureate status would surely change the SBA administrator's mind, or at least begin to raise some questions at the senior staff level in the SBA, so that the job-generation issue could be debated openly. I made copies of the article, passed it around to the staff and brass, and waited. No one in the SBA asked me about Friedman's critique or felt that the Office of Advocacy needed to respond when I raised the issue at a staff meeting.

Although I had addressed my memo to Administrator Bowles, I had no assurance that it had been transmitted to him. Thus, I personally passed my memo of May 3, 1993, which included copies of the Friedman and Leonard articles, to a senior member of Administrator Bowles's staff and asked that he give it the Administrator. Some months later, it was handed back to me with the statement that it was unopened and unread.

It was during this period in 1993 that three Census Bureau

research fellows prepared a paper, "Small Business and Job Creation: Dissecting the Myth and Reassessing the Facts." Steven Davis, John Haltiwanger, and Scott Schuh were three young academics on leave from their university and government jobs. As Census Bureau research fellows, they had access to the bureau's annual manufacturing databases; and as the title of their paper indicates, they argued that the claims made by the Office of Advocacy were statistically fallacious. They also compared Advocacy's manufacturing data with their census data and showed that the two results were entirely different.

This Census Bureau paper identified the regression fallacy in the SBA's claims. It argued that the conventional wisdom about the job-creating prowess of small businesses relied on misleading interpretations of the data. This was the same claim I had made when citing Friedman's analysis in my memo to Bowles. Davis, Haltiwanger, and Schuh reported that the Census Bureau's manufacturing data they had studied showed that small plants accounted for the vast majority of job destruction, that survival rates for manufacturing jobs increased sharply with business size, and that smaller firms had higher gross job-creation rates, but not higher net rates. Net rates are the sum of gross job generation less job destruction.

Through the University of Maryland's legal staff, John Haltiwanger made a Freedom of Information Act (FOIA) request to the SBA to obtain my "Job-Generation Data Problems—What the New Administrator Should Be Told" memo.

In passing the FOIA in 1966, Congress had opened up the activities of the executive offices of the federal government to public scrutiny. The FOIA stated that except in cases of national security and for the protection of personal privacy, information available to executive agencies was to be made available upon request as a matter of public policy, even if the study, memo, statistics, or information did not support the agency's position.

The SBA, claiming that my May 3, 1993 memo was biased, refused to provide my analysis officially and formally to the academics interested in the issue of data quality. Obviously, the SBA wanted my paper suppressed, but it was illegal for the SBA to withhold a research document for the reasons it gave the University of Maryland. I discussed legal action with the University of Maryland lawyer involved, but because my paper was mysteriously obtained by the Census Bureau researchers, further FOIA efforts were not deemed useful.

In the fall of 1993, the NBER released Working Paper #4492, Small Business and Job Creation: Dissecting the Myth and Reassessing the Facts, by the Census Bureau Fellows. It is the practice of most academic economists to obtain comments from their colleagues and other interested parties on their work before publication. The Office of Advocacy did everything it could to suppress the NBER paper, calling on the president of the NBER to retract the article (although in no way was the NBER publication an endorsement of the Fellows' findings). As I understand it, NBER's response was that it did not submit its publications for approval by government officials.

Within the federal bureaucracy, the Office of Advocacy exerted pressure to silence the Census Bureau critics. The Census Bureau is part of the U.S. Department of Commerce, and so the Undersecretary of Commerce for Economic Affairs was also pressured to suppress the paper. The Office of Advocacy argued that it was the administration's policy that small business creates all the jobs, that the Undersecretary of Commerce should become a team player, and that he should repudiate the Census Bureau researchers. To the undersecretary's credit, he refused to do so.

The SBA's Propaganda Machine

The Office of Advocacy continued to try to misinform both business writers who were also trying to get at the truth and frustrated, highly placed government economists who wanted to deal with the SBA's misleading propaganda.

The Council of Economic Advisors (CEA) prepares an annual report, the *Economic Report of the President,* and usually releases it a few days after the president's state of the union address in January. The report articulates the administration's official positions on major economic issues. The usual CEA practice is to ask the executive agencies for comments on early drafts.

Professor William Dickens, a senior economist at the CEA, and now with the Brookings Institution, put together an analysis of the job-generation issue that was highly critical of the SBA's position. I have not seen the CEA draft, but I have been told that the findings of the Census Bureau researchers formed the basis of the CEA report.

This did not sit well with the SBA administrator or the Office of Advocacy. In the fall of 1993, SBA Administrator Bowles, and later the White House Chief of Staff, wrote a letter to the CEA chairperson, asking that the CEA's analysis of the job-generation issue be dropped because the job-generation data were subject to academic "interpretation." The

CEA draft debunking the Office of Advocacy on the job-generation issue did not appear in the February 1994 CEA report.

That action could not have come at a better time to provide NFIB and the small business lobby ammunition they could use to help kill the Clinton administration's health care reform proposals, which were soon to be presented to Congress.

I believe that health care reform, which would have mandated employer-provided health care, was killed by the small business lobby using the job-generation argument. There was no political support for a radical change in health care, such as the Canadian national health insurance plan. The only alternative was to enact an employer mandate. In 1994, more than 40 million Americans were without health insurance. The Clinton administration's health care reform package—whose centerpiece was universal coverage—could be achieved only by an employer mandate. That proposal quickly lost support when a massive lobbying effort was launched that predicted that many employees would lose their jobs if the mandate passed. To support the mandate solution was to kill the goose that laid the golden egg. The mantra, "Small business creates all the jobs," was repeated again and again as support for the health proposal dwindled.

Recall President Clinton in his 1994 state of the union address taking a pen from his pocket, holding it up, and stating that if the health reform package did not cover every American, he would veto it. Today, health care coverage for all Americans is not on anyone's agenda. We are still the only industrial nation where all citizens are not covered by health insurance.

It is important to underscore the utility of the job-generation argument. In a *Washington Post* article on August 21,

1994, Charles Lewis, head of the Center for Public Integrity, observed:

> Whatever you think about health care reform, it is useful to know that a single group, the National Federation of Independent Business (NFIB), has successfully devoted two thirds of its annual budget, about $40 million, to killing the "employer mandate" business tax to finance health care reform. According to John Motley, NFIB's legislative director, "I see us . . . the small business community, the opposing forces, in a position having between 55 and 60 votes in the Senate. Not controlling but having." And no one disputes that assertion.

In July 1994, an NFIB economist and two Office of Advocacy economists presented a paper, "Small Business Job Creation: The Findings and Their Critics," at a meeting of the National Association of Business Economists. The paper was later published in the association's journal, *Business Economics*. The article supported the Office of Advocacy's position, but it provided no data that statisticians or economists could evaluate or could use to make an informed judgment.

Census Bureau data became available in the summer of 1994, but these employment firm size data for 1989-91 were not mentioned, published, or made available to the research community. It was deliberate Office of Advocacy policy to withhold the statistics from those most interested.

Nevertheless, I prepared a paper that showed that large businesses created all the jobs and that small businesses were, in fact, job destroyers.

At an Office of Advocacy conference of academics in September 1994, the Chief Counsel for the Office of Advocacy reported that small business created 91 percent of jobs in the 1989-91 period. These academics (all of whom had published papers on small business issues) immediately asked to see the basic data. The chief counsel responded that it was doing work on the problem and was not ready to release the data because they were preliminary. Yet the data had been obtained months before and had been carefully checked with previously published Census Bureau data. Papers that discussed the job-generation claims were also available. These included my own paper. Advocacy officials were aware of my analysis, which I had personally submitted to the SBA's administrator.

It is illegal for a federal government agency to lobby Congress. Yet this is the Office of Advocacy's purpose. If economic research is conducted by an advocacy organization, and there is no independent review by competent statisticians, the credibility of the government is destroyed. Such an issue should become a matter of public policy.

The Popular Press

In late 1993 and early 1994, several articles about the job-generation issue appeared in newspapers and magazines, including Susan Dentzer's "Doing the Small-Business Shuffle" which appeared in *U.S. News & World Report* (8/16/93). On May 23, 1994, *Barron's* Gene Epstein published a full-page story, "The Real Engine of U.S. Employment Growth Might Be Bigger Than Many Believe." This *Barron's* piece was comprehensive. It quoted the Census Bureau research fellows, enabling them to make a fairly detailed case, and it also illustrated the regression fallacy.

John Haltiwanger, quoted in *Barron's*, summarized the issue in the following way:

> Net job creation behavior in the U.S. manufacturing sector exhibits no strong or simple relationship to employer size. Indeed, this was the very period of massive downsizing in the manufacturing sector. So, finding that large businesses created more than half the jobs is a striking finding.

In June 1994, the Office of Advocacy responded by erroneously claiming that the Census Bureau study showed "that small manufacturers created a disproportionate share of gross and net employment over the sixteen years studied." In September 1994, the SBA's in-house publication, The Small Business Advocate, carried the lead article "Small Business Job Generation: From Revolutionary Idea to Proven Fact." That article ringingly endorsed the Office of Advocacy's earlier distorted propaganda.

The Small Business Advocate noted that the Census Bureau was "developing longitudinal data sets that should allow a more detailed examination of job generation dynamics." In fact, as I have noted, these data had been available for months. A week later, on September 30, 1994, an SBA news release reported, "These figures clearly show that micro-business, not large businesses, create the jobs in our economy." This was a reference to the Census Bureau's data for the 1989-91 period, which had suddenly been made available.

Although no evidence was then cited, the Office of Advocacy has argued in other press releases that the new jobs created by micro-business, firms with less than five employees, were generally permanent, were well paying, and provided good benefits. In *Employers Large and Small* (1990), an extensive and careful analysis of these issues, Charles Brown, James Hamilton, and James Medoff contradicted these assertions.

The September 30, 1994, press release goes on to argue: "These businesses [i.e., micro-businesses] have staying power. They just don't start up and disappear." That assertion is not true. About 840,000, or 16 percent, of businesses with employees terminate each year. My October 1994 article, "On the Formation of Business Firms," in the Monthly Labor Review, showed how economic forces affected quarterly trends in firm formation and termination and illustrated how volatile firm formations and terminations are.

Coincidently, an article in that same *Monthly Labor Review,* by William Wiatrowski, titled "Small Businesses and Their Employees," provides a host of tables, charts, and graphs indicating that small business establishments lay off workers at faster rates during recessions, pay their workers less, and provide fewer benefits.

Other statements from the Office of Advocacy in news releases and other reports reinforce the proposition that small businesses created over 90 percent of jobs. The implication of the Office of Advocacy is that small businesses are the saviors for those seeking jobs.

The statement that small business creates the majority of jobs was contradicted by information published by the Office of Advocacy. Its "Business Answer Card, 1991" reported that for 1984-88, the major period of the Reagan expansion, small businesses "provided 48.5 percent of all new jobs." It also reported that "58 percent of the private workforce" was in small businesses.

Why did the SBA's data contradict their claim? The SBA's regression fallacy was still biasing the data in favor of small businesses. But during this period, almost 11 million jobs were created mostly by large business. The job bias due to the SBA's regression fallacy did not affect the conclusion that large businesses were creating the majority of jobs.

What actually occurred during 1984-88? As in other periods of rapid employment growth, the Office of Advocacy's biased counting methodology was overwhelmed by data from the large business sectors that really were creating jobs. The small business job-generation claim cannot legitimately be made for 1984-88 because large businesses created the overwhelming number of jobs in that period. It is for this reason that David Birch could state, "I can change that number [the small business job-creation rate] at will by changing the starting point or the interval."

The facts, however, have not muted the Office of Advocacy's job-generation drumbeat. A careful analysis of the Census Bureau's data for 1989-91 will show not only that these Office of Advocacy statements are misleading, but that the small business employment share actually declined. Moreover, small businesses lost jobs at a significantly higher rate than large businesses. That is, if we ask what happened to employment in 1991 in small and large firms that employed workers in 1989, the data will show that, in the last recession, small firms lost the overwhelming number of jobs and that the true job creators were large firms.

Chapter 3

The Regression Fallacy

What Is Really Happening to Small and Large Firms?

The SBA's Office of Advocacy counts jobs in a misleading way, and the results it gets from its job-count data are statistically fallacious. To return to our old analogy, the situation is somewhat like going to the race track. You buy an $80 betting ticket, bet $10 on each race, and collect only $65. When you arrive home, your spouse asks how you did. You don't say that you lost $15, but that you won $65.

Next week, you again go to the race track. You once more buy an $80 ticket, but this time you collect $85. Again, your spouse asks you how you did. You don't say that you won $5, but that you won $85.

Unfortunately, this is a lot like the Office of Advocacy's

counting rules. These rules attribute employment gains to small businesses, but attribute employment losses to large businesses. In this way, the Office of Advocacy can claim that small business is creating all the jobs—even though the distribution of firms has remained unchanged for decades.

Regression to the Mean

The regression fallacy has a long history. First, we must understand the statistical use of the term "regression." In 1869, Francis Galton studied various inherited biological traits and noted the relationship between the heights of fathers and their sons. Tall fathers, he observed, tend to have tall sons, and short fathers tend to have short sons. Galton's data are reproduced in M.G. Kendall, *The Advanced Theory of Statistics,* vol. 1 (London: Charles Griffin, 1948), p. 327.

Galton also found that the heights of fathers and their sons are related in a way that we call a statistical regression: In other words, sons of tall fathers are on average shorter than their fathers, and the sons of short fathers are on average taller than their fathers. Galton called these observations a regression to the mean. Galton observed this regression in many areas, and he stated this in a universal law of regression. Statisticians now use the term "regression" to describe the relationship between two or more variables and how they track each other.

We can examine the phenomenon of regression to the mean (small becomes large and large becomes small) in terms of profits. Several studies have compared firms in two periods. In these studies, the firms that were more profitable in the first period generally earned lower profits in the second period while firms that were less profitable in the first period generally reported higher profits in the second period. Of course, some firms prospered or did poorly in both periods, but what is at issue is averages.

Knowledge of regression to the mean has even been used to succeed in the stock market. A financial institution recently recommended the following investment strategy: Divide the money you have to invest into five equal parts. At the beginning of each year (not necessarily the start of a calendar year), buy the five Dow Jones stocks with the lowest price-earnings ratios—in other words, the stocks of the five most out-of-favor companies. One year later, exchange the stocks of companies that are no longer in the bottom five for stocks of the new bottom-five companies. It does not matter which time of the year is selected as the starting date, so long as 12 months go by before the stocks are exchanged. Over the years, this strategy has produced returns that are significantly higher than the Dow Jones. As far as I can determine, this mechanical approach is the only one that has worked over a long period of time. This approach, however, may not work as well once the word gets out.

The Fallacy

The regression phenomenon can, however, lead to fallacious reasoning. Most college textbooks on statistics warn students of the regression fallacy. *Elementary Statistics* by R. Clay Sprowls, for example, provides several examples. One of his examples concerns profits. Sprowls states:

> The fallacy . . . may best be shown by assuming, not unreasonably, that profits have definite upper and lower limits. Then, if there are any changes at all, all the firms with the higher first-period profits will tend to have lower second-period profits, since their profits cannot be larger; similarly, all the firms

with the lower first-period profits will tend to have higher second-period profits since they cannot have lower ones.

In other words, we cannot take the phenomenon of regression to the mean as an ironclad prediction. It is merely a tendency. To discover the extent to which it applies, we have to look at actual data.

The other prong of the regression fallacy is the fallacy of viewing only *some* of the data in terms of regression to the mean. In our race track example, our betting friend counts his winnings and ignores his losses. The bettor committs the fallacy of looking at the favorable results and ignoring results that are unfavorable.

The SBA does something similar when it reports on firms that had employees in both periods. The SBA's "winners" are the firms that went from small to large. The SBA does not count the "losers," the firms that went from large to small.

In the 1989–91 period, firms that were small and became large added 749,000 jobs. During the same period, firms that were large and became small lost 680,000 jobs. This was a net gain of 69,000 jobs for firms that crossed the boundary between size categories. During the period, overall employment grew by 679,000. Yet firms that remained small in this period lost 192,000 jobs. How then could SBA say that small business created all the jobs? It's easy! The SBA starts with the 749,000 jobs of small firms that became large and subtracts the 192,000 jobs lost by firms that stayed small. The result is 557,000 jobs, which is, of course, 91 percent of 679,000, the total growth in overall employment. Knowingly or unknowingly, the regression fallacy is the use of sleight-of-hand in presenting statistics.

So we see that the claim that small business creates all the jobs cannot stand up under scrutiny because it rests on the "statistical regression fallacy."

Counting Employment in a Dynamic Economy

In a dynamic economy such as ours, the fortunes of companies are constantly changing. The economic system is unordered, unpredictable, and chaotic. Economists, including David Birch, have observed that the best predictor of whether a firm will add workers to its payroll within a two-year period is whether the firm *lost* jobs the preceding two years. Conversely, a good predictor of whether a firm will lay off workers in the next two years is whether it *added* workers in the preceding two years.

In analyzing job generation, the rules of counting are extremely important. The Office of Advocacy classifies all enterprises according to their employment size in their initial year. It defines a small business as one with fewer than 500 employees. If an enterprise crosses a size boundary from the first to the second year, the Office of Advocacy attributes the gain or loss to the category in which the firm was initially classified.

We live, however, in a dynamic economy, and if we label firms *only* by their initial size, we throw away valuable information. Let us assume a firm has 490 employees in the initial period and that it adds 1,000 workers in the next period. Should all the job gain be attributed to the small-firm sector? Alternatively, should that firm be classified as large once it has more than 500 employees? And should every job it adds after crossing this 500 mark be attributed to the small-firm sector? (See Appendix F for a fuller explanation.)

The status of firms is in constant flux. A firm that was classified as small (i.e., with fewer than 500 employees) in 1989 could be classified in 1991 as "dead" (having no payroll), or it could remain small or become large. Counting should throw light on the dynamic nature of our economy rather than obscure it.

If we count employment only according to a firm's initial size, we lose sight of the fact that when a firm enters a new size class, its character changes.

A Unique Situation

Nonetheless, perhaps it would be reasonable to continue to count employment according to a firm's initial size. After all, we always measure economic growth from the initial period. Each month, for example, the Bureau of Labor Statistics reports the change in the number of jobs by industry during the preceding month. It notes which major industries increased and which decreased. In general, this is how we think of job change.

But the analysis of job-generation data by firm size is unique. For one thing, we are measuring something (job generation) by unit (the firm), and these units (i.e., firms) are classified according to two characteristics (large and small business). Furthermore, what is important for our analysis is not job generation by unit but job generation by characteristic. Yet the very thing we are measuring—job generation by unit—can change the way we classify the units according to their characteristics (i.e., large and small firms).

When we measure change, we implicitly assume that the characteristic variable—be it employment, firm size, payroll, productivity, or whatever—is unchanged during the period and that only the values of the data are of interest. The reason the flows of employment size are so complicated to follow is that the firm's size characteristic—the characteristic variable—is changing along with the employment flows.

To put it aonther way, as we measure job generation, we see that small firms can become large and large firms can become small. Do we ignore these changes or should we take them into account? I believe we should incorporate these changes into our analysis. We should state how many jobs were created by small firms that became large and how many were lost by large firms that became small.

Data on Hypothetical and Real Firms

The regression fallacy—sorting firms by size class in a dynamic situation—produces an unacceptable result. Assume a three-year employment history of four firms as shown in Table 3.1.

Focus on firm 1. How would the Office of Advocacy's counting rules report the job-generation statistics? Acme twice crosses the boundary of 500 employees. According to Advocacy's counting rules, Acme adds 100 workers in its second year and loses 100 workers in its third year. The Office of Advocacy would consider firm 1 a small business in its first year and would credit small business with creating 100 jobs. In the next year, the Office of Advocacy would consider firm 1 a large business. When it loses 100 jobs, the large business sector would be charged with a loss of 100 jobs.

Assigning all of firm 1's job growth to small business—its classification in year 1—is unsound. Note that there is no change in structure during the entire period. The employment distribution is the same in year 1 and year 3.

In *Elementary Statistics,* Sprowls presents several exam-

Table 3.1

Employment Changes in Four Hypothetical Firms

Year	Firm 1	Firm 2	Firm 3	Firm 4
Y1	450	550	200	800
Y2	550	450	800	200
Y3	450	550	200	800

ples of ordering data that vary over time. He then gives the following warning: "The regression phenomenon ... is a statistical characteristic of the way in which the data are ordered. Fallacious arguments from these relationships should be avoided."

How would the Office of Advocacy's counting rules report the job-generation statistics for all of the boundary-crossing firms shown in Table 3.1? Each year, small firms would be erroneously credited with generating 700 jobs, and large firms would be credited with losing 700 jobs. In year 2, "small" firm 1 is credited with generating 100 jobs and "small" firm 3 with 600 jobs. In year 3, "small" firm 2 is credited with generating 100 jobs and "small" firm 4 with 600 jobs.

Obviously, those 700 new jobs would be a measure of employment volatility, not job generation.

One additional important observation: if the number of stable firms similar to firms 1 and 2 exceeds the number of dynamic firms such as firms 3 and 4, then the job-generation number would be lower than if the reverse is true.

What about the actual job data for 1989-91? What do these data show for firms that changed employment-size categories—that is, for firms that went from small (fewer than 500 employees) to large (500 or more employees), and from large to small? As in the hypothetical firms in Table 3.1, the job change flows cancel each other out statistically. As I stated earlier in this chapter, firms that were small in 1989 but large in 1991 added 749,000 jobs to the U.S workforce while firms that were large in 1989 but small in 1991 lost 680,000 jobs to the U.S. workforce. The net change was an addition of 69,000 jobs. On average over a two-year period our economy produces 4 million jobs. Nonfarm employment in 1979 was 70.9 million and in 1996 was 119.5 million, a gain of almost 50 million in 27 years.

Earlier in this chapter, in explaining the regression fallacy, I discussed the Office of Advocacy's treatment of these data. To recapitulate, the SBA added the 749,000 jobs of small firms that became large and subtracted the 192,000 jobs lost by firms that stayed small. The result—557,000 jobs—was then viewed as the number of jobs created by small business. That is simply misleading. But it would be equally misleading to say that small business lost 680,000 jobs, if we define firm size by the latter period, for a total of 872,000 jobs lost by small business. Milton Friedman now has his answer when he observes, "I have yet to see what the data show if firms are classified by their terminal size."

Several economists have used data from individual firms to assess job-creation issues and have directly questioned the validity of the Office of Advocacy's approach. All have specifically designed other formulations to deal with the regression fallacy problem. Their works are listed in the Bibliography.

The Volatility of Small Firms

Smaller firms are more volatile than the larger firms. Therefore, in a recession period, when few jobs are being created, the

Office of Advocacy—using its job-counting rules—will usually report that small firms create the greatest number of jobs even when small firms are destroying jobs. That is why economist David Birch can state (as quoted in Chapter 2) that he can produce any statistical result he wants by selecting the time frame.

Those who insist that one must count jobs by size of firm in the initial period may be surprised by the employment changes of small and large firms from 1989 to 1991. These data will be discussed in detail in a later chapter, but a few words here may be helpful.

During the 1989-91 recession, workers were four times more likely to lose their jobs if they worked in a small firm than if they worked in a large one. This is indeed surprising information. Most of us think that large firms, on average, have lost jobs at a greater rate than small firms. After all, this is the age of corporate downsizing.

How can our misconceptions be explained? As in an optical illusion, there is a disconnect between the actual data and what we perceive as being significant in that data. And our institutions—particularly the media and Wall Street—play an important role in interpreting data for us.

For example, although large firms have significantly more stable employment levels than smaller firms and although many large firms are adding workers to their payrolls, our daily newspapers headline the downsizing of large firms. And Wall Street pays attention. When a firm announces a downsizing, its stock usually goes up in price. It might not remain higher but initially it rises. In 1995, two large banks announced that they would merge and that 14,000 jobs would be cut; the stock prices of both companies jumped. But the issue is not whether, after these corporate announcements, their stock spikes up and then quickly drops. The point is that after these announcements the company's stock rises.

Actually, no matter what the topic, the media pays attention whenever large numbers are involved. For example, in the last several years, a few tragic airline crashes received significant press space. Yet some 40,000 Americans die each year in car crashes—many more than in those airline crashes combined. However, unless there is some special circumstance (inordinate traffic delays, partying teenagers on prom night, or a celebrity involved), these incidents are rarely reported in our local newspaper or local newscast.

Whenever I discuss the issue of jobs and economic security with non-economists, they mention the planned layoff of 40,000 workers at AT&T. They have no idea that more than 840,000 small firms that employed workers in 1994 employed no workers in 1995.*

If we really want to understand what is going on in both small and large firms, we need to measure the processes of job generation and job loss in a way that is accurate and helpful. It is important to know what the data tell us. I cannot say whether a tree crashing in an uninhabited forest makes a sound. I do know that if no one enters the forest, that tree will never be made into firewood. And if we do not look at our data on job generation and job loss in an objective way, we will not be able to use that data to make good choices for our economy.

---

*See my article in the *Monthly Labor Review,* October 1994, for a discussion of historical trends in firm formation and dissolution.

Chapter 4

Job Creation by Firm Size

What the New Census Bureau Data Tell Us

When we hear the term "small business," we are likely to think of the mom-and-pop carry-out near our office, the neighborhood convenience store where we sometimes pick up a few items, the garage that has taken such good care of our car for years. Just the term "small business" may evoke a warm, fuzzy feeling for those of us whose parents or grandparents ran a small business.

Yet which firms employ the most people—small or large businesses? Do government policies that favor small businesses really help the ordinary person? And are such policies justified?

The U.S. economy encompasses more than 5 million firms. However, fewer than 14,000 of the largest U.S. firms (with 500 or more employees) employ 42 percent of the workforce. Why is the distribution of employment so concentrated in a relatively few large firms? This situation occurs not only in the United States; it has been observed across all major countries and most industries. Some underlying process must be at work. Until now, however, no comprehensive longitudinal data for firms were accessible to explain it.*

The newly available data—longitudinal Census Bureau data for the entire nonfarm workforce sector—can provide important insights into both job generation and the distribution of employment by firm size. The data show the dynamic process of the growth and decline of employment by size of firm.

How the New Data Originated

The Internal Revenue Service (IRS) requires all firms with employees to file quarterly payroll reports. These reports provide comprehensive data for the private nonfarm sector, enabling the IRS to keep track of payroll deductions for Social Security and federal income taxes. Under long-standing arrangements, the Census Bureau obtains these data for its annual County Business Pattern program and its periodic industrial censuses.

The Census Bureau combines the IRS quarterly payroll reports with its own annual Company Organization Survey of

---

*This kind of concentration is also called the Pareto distribution, a term usually used to describe the statistical distribution of income and wealth, which are also highly concentrated.

all large multi-establishment firms to form its Standard Statistical Establishment List (SSEL). The two sets of data are easy to combine since firms are identified by their Employer Identification Number (EIN) in both.

At my request (see Chapter 1), the Census Bureau used its 1989 and 1991 SSEL files to tabulate employment data by firm size. In accord with my specifications (see Appendix B), the Census Bureau added together all the establishments for multi-establishment companies (obtained from its Company Organization Survey) and cross-tabulated the data by firm-size class (obtained from the IRS payroll data). The resulting tabulation showed—in matrix form—the employment status of workers in the private nonfarm sector by major industry division and firm size for both 1989 and 1991, the number of firms in each class, and in addition, annual payrolls for both periods.

Problems of Definition and Measurement

We all know what a job is. Yet the everyday definition of a job may not coincide with the Census Bureau's. To measure jobs, the Census Bureau counts all people on the payroll at the mid-March reporting period. It does not differentiate between part-time and full-time employment and does not count unfilled vacancies as jobs.

When we speak of jobs generated by small business, we need to know what definition of small business is being used. For research purposes, a small business is a legal entity employing fewer than 500 workers. SBA researchers are encouraged to use this measure, unless there is an overriding reason not to do so. In contrast, for program purposes, the SBA arbitrarily defines small businesses in relation to the industry structure and with an eye on the size of firms that would be excluded from special procurement opportunities and guaranteed loan activities.

The Census Bureau SSEL data are ideal for measuring job generation because employment changes for firms can be followed for a considerable time. In addition, the entry and exit of firms can be identified. A report with a new EIN—one that did not previously appear in the file—indicates the birth of a firm, and an old report with no payroll in the most recent period indicates the death of a firm.

To thoroughly understand the process of job generation, however, we need to consider some areas the Census Bureau does not currently cover. The Census Bureau data, for example, do not include the growing number of self-employed people who do contract work for businesses of various sizes. And one of the fastest growing industries, "employee leasing," is not really an industry, but a legal form of employee-employer relationship. Should employees involved in employee leasing be counted as employees of the firm to which they are leased or as employees of the leasing agency? The question is moot because the statistical agencies are unable to obtain information to allocate leased workers to the industry of employment.

Franchising also poses a classification issue. By definition, a small business is both below a certain size as well as independently owned and operated. If a large franchisor dictates the way its franchisees operate their businesses, should those franchised businesses be classified as small, as the Census Bureau now classifies them?

Furthermore, the Census Bureau data do not readily measure the impact of mergers, acquisitions, divestitures, and reorganizations. Since firms generally merge with other firms in their size class, this probably causes little distortion.

The Census Bureau data do not address the underground economy. Its data do not count illegal activity, nor do they count the legal activities of employees that are not reported to the IRS.

If resources are made available, the Census Bureau can—if it is willing to cooperate—analyze in detail several of the methodological issues raised above.

Remarkable Stabilities: Employment Distributions by Establishment Size

In gathering employment statistics, federal agencies focus on detailed industries and small geographic areas. To get the information they need, federal agencies require firms to report their data by work sites or establishments. This does not create a problem for single-establishment firms because for them there is no difference between firm and establishment. A large firm, however, may have many small establishments, sometimes several thousand. Distributions of small establishments, therefore, are not synonymous with distributions of small firms. With this caveat, we can draw inferences from the establishment series.

Major economic changes have occurred since World War II. Nonetheless, when Census Bureau data for establishments are examined by employment size, there appears to have been no change in the employment size structure since 1946. (See Appendix E for the data.) Unfortunately, no long-term comprehensive data by firm size that better suit our analytical needs are available for the postwar period, until 1982.

Employment Distributions by Firm Size

The Census Bureau has recently made employment data available by firm size for 1982-87 and 1989-91. These data confirm that there has been no basic change in the size distribution of firms during these periods.

Furthermore, a remarkable statistical result is evident—a firm has the same probability of adding employees as of losing them.

For 1982-87, the Census Bureau tabulated data by firm size for firms whose employment increased or decreased. These tabulations were based on a 2-percent random sample. Initially, the 1982-87 Census Bureau tabulations were structured in such a way that employment data could not be released because of confidentiality provisions.

Census Bureau data for subsequent periods were significantly richer and were not based on a sample. For 1989-91, the Census Bureau provided the data in matrix form. That is, it prepared tables that reported the number of firms by size in 1989 cross-classified by their size in 1991. In addition, the Census Bureau tabulated employment and payroll data by industry and firm size for both years.

The Census Bureau's employment-size data tabulations are totally comparable with its published County Business Pattern data for 1989 and 1991.

In spite of the dynamic changes in firm size for individual firms, firm size does not affect whether a firm will increase or decrease its employment. In fact, tabulations of data on firm employment from the Census Bureau reveal that firms with five or more employees in both 1989 and 1991 had an equal probability of increasing or decreasing their employment from 1989 to 1991. Furthermore, a firm with ten employees had the same probability of increasing (or decreasing) its employment as a firm with 2,000 employees.

Moreover, when the data are analyzed, the size distribution of firms in 1993 will remain unchanged if the pattern of change in the 1989–91 period continues. If we assume that births are the same in 1991 and 1993 and we compute the distributions of matrix changes for 1993 with the use of the 1989–91 probabilities, the employment size distribution of firms will not change.

Because the same number of firms is shifting from large to small as from small to large, the U.S. economy is in a dynamic steady state. The economy is dynamic in the sense that the system is expanding, but it is steady in the sense that the distribution is unchanging.

Job Creation by Firm Size

The SBA's Office of Advocacy has assumed that comparing the beginning and end years' employment distribution would distort the contribution of small firms. According to the Office of Advocacy, this would occur because the contribution of small firms that grew into large firms would understate the contribution of small firms to the job-generation process. Is this indeed the case? My analysis shows otherwise.

The period under consideration—March 1989 to March

1991—was one of the slowest periods of job growth since World War II. The private nonfarm sector added 679,000 workers in this period, whereas the average growth in the preceding 30 years was nearly 2 million per year.

Yet large and small firms did not fare equally well in job creation during this two-year period. Cross-sectional global data for all U.S. firms show that small businesses lost 353,000 jobs (49,354,000 minus 49,001,000) and large businesses gained 1,032,000 jobs (43,304,000 minus 42,272,000). (See Appendix G, Table G.1).

In other words, small businesses employed 353,000 fewer workers in 1991 than in 1989. Large businesses, on the other hand, added 1,032,000 workers to their payrolls during this period.

For the first time, we can learn how these employment changes affected the distribution of employment by firm size. A total of 12 employment data values is involved. We count the number of workers who were added to small and large firms that remained in the same size class in both years (4 values), and we account for the employment changes in firms that changed their size class from 1989 to 1991 (4 values). In addition, we count the number of employees in 1989 in small and large firms that went out of business by 1991 (deaths) and the number of employees that were employed by new small and large firms in 1991 (births; 4 values).

To simplify the discussion, I counted, as does the Office of Advocacy, employment gains in firms born in 1991 as being in the small size category in 1989—that is, as if the firms existed in 1989 but had no employees then. If the firms born in 1991 were small, I counted their employment in the small category in 1991. If they were large, I counted their employment in the large category in 1991.

In mirror-image fashion, I counted employment for firms that died by 1991 in the small category if the firms were small in 1989. If they were large in 1989, I put them in the large-firm category. I show births and deaths separately in the tables below.

To simplify this information, it is necessary to reduce the problem to four numbers as shown below (see the following tables). For firms that remained small in both periods, Table 4.1 provides the relevant data. We see that firms that were small in both periods employed 192,000 fewer workers in 1991. For firms that remained large in both periods, Table 4.2 provides the relevant data. Note that births or deaths are not applicable by definition. In Table 4.3, we see that employment in small firms that became large increased 749,000. And in Table 4.4, we can see that employment in large firms that became small decreased 680,000. These figures are statistically almost a mirror image of the 749,000 that were small in 1989 and large in 1991, as reported in Table 4.3.

The net employment changes are summarized in Table 4.5. The component change, or the change in employment between 1989 and 1991, was 679,000 workers. That is, the net job losses and job gains from Tables 4.1 through 4.4 sum to 679,000, the total job gain for this period.

What does Table 4.5 tell us? In simple terms, firms that remained small lost 192,000 jobs during 1989-91. During that period, large businesses added 802,000 workers to their payrolls. Employment gains of firms going from small to large

Table 4.1

Employment in Firms That Remained Small in 1989 and 1991

1989 employment 48,726,000 (includes 8,334,000 deaths)
1991 employment 48,534,000 (includes 6,366,000 births)
Net loss −192,000

Note: Deaths: There were 8,334,000 workers in small firms in 1989 who were gone by 1991. They are deaths because they were employed in firms that no longer existed in 1991. Births: In 1991, there were 6,366,000 workers in firms that did not exist in 1989.

Table 4.2

Employment in Firms That Remained Large in 1989 and 1991

1989 employment 41,125,000 (includes 1,147,000 deaths)
1991 employment 41,927,000 (includes 1,472,000 births)
Net gain 802,000

Note: Births and deaths are shown separately in order to show later how the SBA computes its 91 percent job-generation numbers.

Table 4.3

Employment in Firms That Were Small in 1989 and Large in 1991

1989 employment 628,000
1991 employment 1,377,000
Net gain 749,000

Table 4.4

Employment in Firms That Were Large in 1989 and Small in 1991

1989 employment	1,147,000
1991 employment	467,000
Net loss	−680,000

Table 4.5

Net Employment Change by Size of Firm in 1989 and Size of Firm in 1991

Type of Firm	Small in 1991	Large in 1991
Small in 1989	−192,000	749,000
Large in 1989	−680,000	802,000
Net gain		679,000

were about offset by employment losses of firms that were large and became small.

This contradicts everything the SBA's Office of Advocacy reported.

Instead, we find that the two employment flows are approximately symmetrical. That is, the number of firms that were small in the initial year and became large in the later year about equaled the number of firms that were large in the initial year and became small in the terminal year. This observation is also consistent with Census Bureau data for a different period—1982-87—that showed that the same number of firms increased employment as decreased employment.

The Regression Fallacy at Work

We can see how the regression fallacy works in Table 4.6.

The SBA has reported 557,000 as the number of jobs

Table 4.6

The Regression Fallacy at Work

Status		Employment		Jobs created by firms that were small businesses in	
1989	1991	1989	1991	1989	1991
Small	Small	48,726	48,534	−192	−192
Small	Large	628	1,377	749	NA
Large	Small	1,147	467	NA	−680
Job creation by small firms in 1989				557	
Job creation by small firms in 1991					−872

Sources: Tables 4.1, 4.3, and 4.4.

created by small business. To get this figure, the SBA counted the jobs lost by small firms (−192,000) and added the jobs gained by small firms that became large (749,000). These data are reported in Tables 4.1 through 4-4.

If we assume that size, using 1991 controls, an approach that is just as logical, then total net job creation by small business between 1989 and 1991 was -872,000 jobs. Identifying firms in this way would mean that small firms lost 872,000 jobs. The SBA has not reported this figure.

Milton Friedman now has the answer to his question of what happens when employment change is measured using the firm size at the end of the period. Obviously, small business cannot gain 557,000 jobs while simultaneously losing 872,000 jobs. Such a result would be sheer nonsense.

The counting rule used by the SBA's Office of Advocacy ignores the fact that a firm changes its characteristic when it changes from one size class to another. This changing characteristic adds a unique dimension to the problem of measuring job generation by employment size (see Chapter 3).

Those who argue that one must count jobs by size of firm in the initial year may be surprised to learn what happened to small firm employment from 1989 to 1991 for firms with fewer than 500 workers in 1989. Note that the focus is on firms that existed in 1989. For those firms, essentially ignoring births, what has happened to their employment in 1991. A simple calculation from the Census Bureau data shows that such firms employed 5,809,000 fewer workers in 1991. (To get this figure, add the net changes of Tables 4.1 and 4.3 and subtract jobs for births of both large and small firms.)

In contrast, large firms with 500 or more employees in 1989 reported job losses of only 1,345,000 during 1989-91. Table 4.2 shows that firms that were large in 1989 and 1991 added 992,000 workers. Table 4.4 shows that firms that were large in 1989 and became small in 1991 lost 2,342,000 workers.

What are the results in percentage terms for firms that reported employees in 1989? Small firms lost 12 percent of their positions by 1991; large firms lost only 3 percent by 1991. Thus, we see that employment is four times as stable in large firms as in small firms.

The area of concern is in the treatment of employment in firms that changed size category from 1989 to 1991. If an overwhelming number of small firms became large over this period, then cross-sectional statistics would understate the contribution of small business to the job-generation process.

Contrary to fact, assume an economy where a significant number of small firms in 1989 became large in 1991 and where no firms that were large in 1989 became small in 1991. If the distributions alone were analyzed, it would appear that employment growth was taking place in large companies and that small companies were not growing. Then one could argue that the true job-generation contribution of small companies was being underreported.

In fact, the Census Bureau data show that, on net, we have approximately the same numbers of workers (and firms) going from large to small as from small to large. On net, firms that were small in 1989 but became large in 1991 gained virtually the same number of jobs (749,000 equals 1,377,000 minus 628,000) as did firms that were large in 1989 but became small in 1991 (680,000 equals 1,147,000 minus 467,000).

Because the gross flows among size groups are similar in terms of both firms and employment, the measure of job generation under these circumstances is the change in the distribution of employment in the two years.

Advocacy economists measure the job-generation contribution of small firms by first taking the sum of all workers in 1991 who worked in small firms in 1989. This figure is 43,546,000 (42,169,000 were in small firms in 1991, and 1,377,000 were in firms that were small in 1989 but large in 1991). Next they subtract 49,354,000 workers who were in small firms in 1989. Then they add 6,366,000 small firm births in 1991.

In a memorandum to the National Association of Business Economists (circa fall of 1994), the SBA's Office of Advocacy described its methodology:

> The "size distribution fallacy" . . . is of academic interest, but has little practical relevance. . . . For 1989-1991 the "gross flow" employment movements during that period may be sum-

marized as follows: jobs created by small firms which remained small from 1989-1991—1.86 million; jobs created by new small births—6.44 million; jobs created by firms which were small in 1989 but large in 1991 (i.e., boundary crossers)—807 thousand. In other words, of the 8.93 million gross jobs created by small firms between 1989 and 1991, 807 thousand—or 9.0 percent came from the "regression fallacy." Looked at another way, 771 thousand jobs were also lost by large firms which became small in 1991. In other words, the boundary crossers almost netted each other out, and are not relevant because they are such a small source of employment growth.

The numbers quoted above were based on a preliminary Census Bureau 2–percent sample of firms. Furthermore, the above statement is deliberately misleading. Small firms that remained small lost 192,000 jobs. They did not create 1.86 million jobs. It is obvious that small businesses did not create 8.93 million jobs during this period. Simply put, the 8.3 million small firm job loss from firm deaths is omitted from the statistics; *all* firms added about 679,000 jobs.

Is the regression fallacy solely of academic interest, as the SBA economists maintain? In that case, why has the SBA taken pains to keep the data inaccessible to academics and business economists?

Employment Volatility

Previous Census Bureau tabulations for 1982 and 1987 showed that firms with five or more employees—irrespective of size in 1982—had equal probabilities of increasing and of decreasing their employment in 1987. That is, the same number of firms gained employment as lost employment. This is not true of the smallest size class because that size class is bounded by zero, and if a firm with one or two employees lost one or two workers, it would be a death.

In 1991, there were about 1.2 million new firms in the system. *New* here is defined as having no employment in 1989. These firms may be in the process of expanding or they may be basing their decisions on long-term considerations more than other larger and established firms do. Economists in the Bureau of Labor Statistics note that the reason for the downward bias in the monthly establishment employment survey numbers is that newer establishments increase their employment faster than older establishments, but currently there is a considerable time lag before new firms can be included in the sample.

Firm Volatility

What these statistics suggest is an economic world where firms add or lose employment randomly, without regard to their initial size, except for the newest and smallest firms.

Firms grow in their initial startup period. In some firms, employment also grows immediately afterward. Whether such firms continued their growth in subsequent periods is something the Census Bureau data can answer as more comparable annual files become available. Getting such answers by firm size would also add to our knowledge of job creation.

These Census Bureau data show large numbers of firms starting up and large numbers going out of business. This reflects the dynamic nature of our economy as firms expand and contract. However, the resulting statistical symmetry, in employment terms, is truly remarkable as firms adapt to changing economic conditions.

Other data on firm formation and destruction underscore the dynamic character of the American economy. At the end of 1993, there were 5.85 million firms with employees reporting to state employment security offices. More than 911,000 of these were new in that they had no employees in previous years. At the same time, there were 801,000 firms that reported employees in previous years but reported no employees in 1993. This is in line with the Census Bureau data that showed approximately 1,230,000 new firms reporting payrolls in 1991 along with 1,200,000 firms that existed in 1989 but no longer reported payrolls in 1991.

Parenthetically, these findings counter the speculation of some economists that we live in a winner-take-all society. Although income and wages may be growing more disparate, they are doing so because the economic rules of the game are changing: For example, the union power that maintained labor's share of corporate earnings has waned. Marginal tax rates at upper income levels have declined sharply since 1981 (despite increasing slightly in 1994). Growing international competition has put pressure on wages but not on profits or executive salaries. The real minimum wage has eroded, and unemployment insurance (which kept many workers out of poverty during economic downturns) has declined in relation to average wages.

Our daily newspapers feature the downsizing announcements of large firms. They ignore the fact that large firms have significantly more stable employment levels than smaller companies do. Large firms also create more jobs.

The Clinton Administration's Position
Since November 1996

My SLATE article, "Small-Biz Blarney," was published in November 1996. It debunked the job-generation claims of the SBA. Soon afterwards, the mantra, "Small business creates all the jobs," was dropped by White House spokespersons. I do not know why they dropped it, or what the politics were inside the White House, but it was dropped. For six full years, the economy has continued to create jobs at an amazing pace, and since President Clinton's second election the administration has not attributed these gains to small business.

Chapter 5

Explaining the Employment Distribution by Firm Size

The Economic Game

This chapter outlines for economists and statisticians a new approach to the understanding of the size distribution of firms. Those with some knowledge of statistics and economics will find this chapter of interest because it advances economic theory with respect to the size distribution of firms. However, if terms such as steady state systems, probability matrices, and stochastic simulation models are not your forte, you will find this chapter difficult.

For those readers unfamiliar with the statistical jargon, let me briefly summarize the substance of this chapter.

Forty years ago, industrial organization economists proposed a model that "explained" why we have the very concentrated size distribution of firms. These industrial organization economists argued that the concentration of employment in a few large firms is the result of competition among firms. This competition is very much like a gambling game.

The Census Bureau data for 1989–91 show that as a result of this competition half the firms increased their employment during this two-year period and the other half decreased their employment. There has been no change in the distribution by business size since 1946, and the reason is that constant historic competitive forces among firms have created this distribution. As a result of this competition, about 14,000 firms out of a total population of 5 million firms employ almost half the workforce. In contrast to these few successful firms, millions have fallen by the wayside or remained very small.

I use the Census Bureau data for 1989–91 to confirm that this unique data set can be used to define the economic game. By developing a probability model from the Census Bureau data for 1989–91, I show that the competitive economic system generated the current distribution of jobs, just as casino gambling redistributes the gains and losses among participants in accordance with the rules of probability.

The Employment Distribution by Firm Size

Although this chapter does not deal directly with the job-generation hoax, it does explain how our competitive economy really works.

In all industrial countries and in most industries, the distribution of employment is highly skewed (concentrated) by business size.* Most industries consist of a few dominant firms and a large number of very small ones. This phenomenon exists in all free mature economic systems. Recall that in the United States, 45 percent of employment is accounted for by 14,000 large firms; the remaining 55 percent of employment is spread among the 5 million smaller firms. Given that this highly skewed distribution is universal, one would expect some process to be at work to account for it. There is, and the explanation is fascinating.

Economic Theory

Erroneously, economic textbooks usually account for this concentration of employment by explaining that the long-run industry-average cost curve is U-shaped. In other words, in almost any economic venture, average costs by size of firm are at first very high for small quantities of output, then decline as output expands, and eventually turn upward as capacity is strained and the span of control grows unmanageably. However, economists have not satisfactorily explained why this U-shaped cost curve should produce such highly skewed distributions in virtually all industrial sectors.

If, for example, a similar mechanism operated in markets, most firms would cluster about the lowest cost point at which they could maximize their profits. Firms that were too large would shrink, while those that were too small would tend to expand. Yet this does not occur. Firms with a large share of

---

*I am indebted to Herbert Simon and Charles Bonini for their insightful analysis of the issue of the employment distribution by firm size in "The Size Distribution of Business Firms" (*American Economic Review* [September 1958]).

the market usually have no tendency to shrink; they often do quite well.

Economic theory will not predict the size distribution of firms—for either the entire economy or a specific industry. Economic theory does predict that very small firms will be volatile. Either they will expand, grow, and become more efficient, or they will fall by the wayside. Census Bureau data support this observation.

Business Size and Poker

I will show that the distribution of firms by size of employment is indeed the result of a business gaming model. That is, with several important exceptions, the distribution of winnings for the business game—sales, profits, employment—is somewhat like the outcome of a classic poker tournament. The poker game and the economic game create the distribution of wealth and employment.

When the poker tournament starts, we cannot predict which individual poker player might win, but we can predict that there will be one winner. The same holds true for the business "game." Although we cannot predict the winners and losers, we know that some firms will be winners and others losers. And if we know the parameters of the business gaming model, we can predict the size distribution of industry activity. By labeling this process a "game," I do not mean to belittle its seriousness.

Major poker tournaments often begin with 36 tables of 6 players each, a total of 216 players, who enter with a fixed amount of cash, usually several thousand dollars. Each player has an equal chance of winning any one hand of poker. However, ultimately there will be one winner at each table. The first round ends when one player wins all the money at risk at his or her table. Each of these winners goes on to the second round, which begins with 6 tables of 6 players, for a total of 36 players. Again, play ends at each table when one player wins all the money at risk. These 6 winning players compete in the final round, and the tournament ends when one person has won all the money at risk.

Although the business "game" resembles a poker tournament, there are important differences. In the poker tournament, everyone must compete from the beginning. In the economic system, firms are constantly being "born" into the system. In the poker tournament, all players have the same size stake, but in business competition, firms start with investments of differing amounts. Another distinction is that in the economy, with free entry and the ability of firms to merge, the employment distribution will become stable. Furthermore, no one firm can legally exert a permanent monopoly.

In addition, large firms, defined here as employing 500 or more employees, do not necessarily compete with each other. A large automobile producer does not compete with a large software firm or with a large hospital or utility. Furthermore, other factors come into play: patents have a fixed life; regulated utilities are limited in their geographic scope; innovation and technological change are constantly at work to reduce the profits of monopolies or oligopolies.

In a nation's economy, one firm does not accumulate all the wealth. Unlike the situation in the poker tournament, if many new firms continually enter the system there will be no ultimate winner. Recall that 1.2 million firms of the 5 million smallest U.S. firms were new in that they had no employees two years before.

The Workings of Random Statistical Chance

What happens if one assumes that dynamic and volatile changes are indeed taking place among firms, but that size does not affect the probability that a firm will grow or decline?

Several economists who specialize in industrial organizational theory have hypothesized that the size distribution of employment is the result of pure historical chance. In other words, the size distribution of employment occurs by random statistical chance very similar to the chance that causes the winnings at a poker table to be redistributed.

Let us assume that firms grow or decline depending on such factors as profit, managerial efficiency, industry trends, regional trends, management expertise, consumer preferences, the ability to obtain financial assistance, and the ability to adapt to technological change. Let us also assume that in statistical terms, this process is both random and independent—that is, that previous performance has little relation to future performance. We then have a situation that is similar to tossing a coin, playing dice, or playing poker.

Simon and Bonini's Simulation Approach

Herbert Simon and Charles Bonini, aware of the empirical shortcomings of the economic theorists, have proposed a novel approach to the problem. They argue that a business gaming model best explains the forces that have generated the dynamic structure that characterizes the U.S. economy.

To illustrate this point, they assume that a new industry comes into existence with 50 firms, each with a 2-percent share of the market. Although average industry growth is rapid and fixed, firms grow in random fashion. That is, for each period, half the firms will be lucky and grow faster than average, while half the firms will be unlucky and grow slower than average. I use the concept of luck in the same way as the athlete who says, "The harder I practice, the luckier I get." Essentially, for our purposes, however, dice are thrown in this statistical experiment. (In statistical parlance, one "samples from a distribution." Assume a normal distribution of 6 percent and a standard deviation of 16 percent. A standard deviation of 16 percent was selected for this illustration because it represented the standard deviation for the annual change in employment among the Fortune 500 firms in the early postwar period.)

Although each of the 50 firms faces the same probability of growing or declining, its actual growth depends on luck—a random sampling from a probability distribution. When this process continues for a short time, the four firm-concentration ratio—a general measure of industry conglomeration—rapidly approaches 60 percent. In other words, given this experiment, in a short period of time the four largest firms will control 60 percent of the jobs.

This illustration does not mirror actual economic conditions in that it does not take into account mergers and acquisitions or new firm entrants; all of these have a major impact on the distribution. Nevertheless, in industry studies, it is not unusual to find a small number of firms with a large share of the market, while their former competitors muddle along with less than 1 percent of market share. Just as some poker players are better than others, some firms are better managed, can innovate more quickly, have a more productive workforce, and have greater access to capital.

An analysis of this statistical gaming model reveals that once the luckiest or most fortunate firms pull away from the pack, it is difficult for laggards to rally and regain their lost market share.

Gaming Model Assumptions

The simulation experiment reported here assumed that all firms faced the same fixed distribution regardless of size and that their growth rates were independent of the firms' history. These assumptions need not be rigid for the model to reproduce the firm-size employment distributions.

Instead of attempting to create a theory of what should be happening, Simon and Bonini explain what they observe and assert that it is precisely this dynamic gaming process that determines the current industry structure. They report:

> Since published empirical data on the distribution of firms by size are numerous and monotonously similar, we will limit ourselves to some illustrative figures. Whether sales, assets, number of employees, value added, or profits are used as the size measure, the distribution always belongs to a class of highly skewed distributions that include the log-normal and the Yule. This is true for all industries taken together. It holds for sizes of plants as well as of firms.

The Yule distribution assumes that (1) the probability distribution conforms to the law of proportionate effect and (2) new firms come into the economic system at a relatively constant rate. In fact, this is precisely what is occurring. Otherwise one firm would emerge the winner and employ the entire labor force, just as the poker tournament winner wins the entire pot.

Why the Distribution of Employment
Is Universally Concentrated

The Census Bureau's data can be used to demonstrate that our random gaming model of the economy explains why the distribution of firms is highly skewed. In addition, the ongoing nature of the economic process explains why the distribution of firms by size of employment is so universally concentrated.

As I mentioned in Chapter 1, Jonathan Leonard observed that the distribution of employment by firm size has not changed for a considerable period of time.*

The Census Bureau provides data by establishment size beginning with 1946. There appears to be no change in the employment size distribution over time. This can now be explained by the random gaming model.

The Census Bureau tabulations provided data by firm size in 1989, cross-classified by firm size in 1991 and employment in these two years. An analysis of these data explains empirically why the size distribution of firms is not changing. Moreover, the data can be used to create a model of our economy.

As observed in Chapter 4, the job change movements, crossing the boundaries of firm size, are generally mirror images of each other. By the same token, approximately, the same numbers of firms move to larger size classes as move to smaller size classes. These data are shown in Table 5.1.

The data from Table 5.1 indicate the status of firms by size in 1989, cross-classified by firm size in 1991. The table

---

*On the Size Distribution of Employment and Establishments, NBER Working Paper #1951 (New York: National Bureau of Economic Research, 1985). Others have made similar observations for firm size or establishment.

shows, for example, that there were 61,552 firms with 20-49 employees in 1989 that reduced their employment and moved to the 5-19 employment size class in 1991. During that same period, 64,960 firms added employees and moved from 5-19 employees to 20-49 employees. For the most part, the firm shifts are approximate mirror images of each other, except for the smallest firms with 0-4 employees.

My initial request to the Census Bureau was for 1982-87, a period of rapid employment growth. A random 2-percent sample file already existed for these industrial census years. The Census Bureau provided simple counts of firms that increased their employment and decreased their employment by firm employment size. This finding at first was inexplicable. Shortly thereafter, the 1989-91 recession period tabulations became available, and they also showed the same results. That is, an equal number of firms in each size class reported employment gains as reported employment losses.*

For this 1989-91 period, an analysis of the employment shifts between size classes shows that their employment shifts were mirror images of each other. No matter which pair of size classes I selected, I found that the flows across size classes were equal and opposite, irrespective of business-cycle conditions. The probability that a firm will add or lay off workers is equal and independent of size.

A simple economic explanation accounts for these observations. Firms are constantly competing with each other. Jobs are created when there is work to be done. Both small and large businesses try to expand their sales of goods and services to

---

*Appendix G provides detailed data for 1989-91 by size of firm, employment, and payrolls.

Table 5.1

Firm Size in 1989 by Firm Size in 1991 and the Probability Distribution

	1989 Employment size	Not active in 1991	Employment in 1990 [1]					
			0–4	5–19	20–49	50–99	100–499	500 or More
1991 Total	5,051,025							
1989 Total	5,021,315		3,036,304	1,492,595	336,376	103,435	68,338	13,977
Not active in 1989			974,933	192,643	39,546	13,188	8,575	978
Number of Employees								
0–4	3,003,224	864,210	1,822,097	293,680	18,130	3,633	1,406	68
5–19	1,490,651	252,001	229,353	940,833	64,960	2,899	585	20
20–49	339,008	54,070	7,909	61,552	192,395	21,361	1,685	36
50–99	104,951	17,570	1,404	3,036	19,586	53,975	9,331	49
100–499	69,608	11,026	574	809	1,702	8,329	45,499	1,669
500 or more	13,873	1,276	34	42	57	50	1,257	11,157

Percent Distribution

Number of Employees							
0-4	100.00	28.78	60.67	9.78	0.60	0.12	0.05	0.01
5-19	100.00	16.91	15.39	63.12	4.36	0.19	0.04	0.05
20-49	100.00	15.95	2.33	18.16	56.75	6.30	0.50	
50-99	100.00	16.74	1.34	2.89	18.66	51.43	8.89	
100-499	100.00	15.84	0.82	1.16	2.45	11.97	65.36	2.40
500 or more	100.00	9.20	0.25	0.30	0.41	0.36	9.06	80.42

Source: Unites States Bureau of the Census, special tabulations.

increase their profitability. Some are successful, others not. This accounts for the volatility. All the economic research suggests that once a firm grows beyond a minimum size there are no differences in the efficiency between small and large firms.

It is for this reason that when the available Census Bureau data are examined for the last 50 years there is no evidence that there has been any basic change in the employment size distribution of firms and establishments.

Past and Future

How can one explain the employment distribution by firm size? What will happen to the distribution in the future?

Economists have failed to explain this universal concentration of economic activity. As noted previously, the textbook explanation has almost always assumed that a U-shaped long-run marginal cost curve was the basic causal mechanism. Firm size would tend to be optimal. However, there is little satisfactory explanation why this cost curve mechanism produces the very highly skewed distributions observed.

If business forces operated this way, a large number of firms would cluster about the lowest marginal cost point. Those that were too large would become small, while those that were small would tend to grow. This is not what one observes. If the marginal cost curves at large output levels are rising and there are limited returns to scale, why do so many firms with a large share of the market do well?

If we can understand the statistical/economic process, we can get some answers to these questions.

The distribution of firms by size is the result of a fascinating experiment or game. This gaming model creates the distribution we observe. The following illustration of this game best explains the forces that have generated the dynamic economic structure that characterizes the U.S. economy.

We observed that the movements-across-firm-size categories are generally mirror images of each other. Approximately, the same numbers of firms move to larger size classes as move to smaller size classes. (See Table 5.1.) Using the Census Bureau's data for 1989 and 1991, we can compute a probability matrix model. All this means is that we can compute the probability that a firm in a particular employment size class in 1989 will move to another size class in 1991.

The model enables us to answer several specific questions. What will happen in the future? What has happened in the past to get us to this state? And what will happen to the size distribution of firm employment in the future, if the U.S. firm economic history in 1989 and 1991 continues?

The answer to the last question is that nothing will change. The probability matrix describes a steady state process. If the U.S. firm economic history in 1989 and 1991 continues into the future, nothing will change. Obviously some firms will do well and others will shrink, but the distribution will remain essentially unchanged, as it has remained unchanged since 1946.

Another question is what will happen if we start an economy with 5 million small firms, and firms are subject to the same dynamic patterns of size change? To answer this question we start the game in year one when all firms are very small and apply the 1989–91 probability matrix again and again. We redistribute the firms in the initial period using the probability model.

The surprising finding is that in a few short periods of time, firms will distribute themselves in essentially the same way they are distributed currently and have been since 1946.

Just as the DNA of a person predetermines that person's physical characteristics, our firm probability distribution model predicts the future distribution of employment by firm size.

Formation Rates of Business Firms

In a recent paper, "On the Formation of Business Firms," published in the U.S. Department of Labor's Monthly Labor Review (October 1994), I reported on formation rates of business firms. The original data were obtained from state employment security agencies that report to the U.S. Department of Labor's Employment and Training Administration.

An analysis of these data reveals the dynamic nature of the American economy. These data show that the actual gross rates of firm formation are significantly higher than private credit rating companies had previously reported.

The data series starts in 1982. The number of firms has grown by 2 percent per year since then, about the same rate of growth as the workforce. However, the net growth rate masks the volatility of the firm-formation process. Gross rates for new firm formation averaged 16 percent, and gross termination rates averaged 14 percent since 1982.

The actual numbers involved are a measure of economic volatility. At the beginning of 1995, there were more than 6 million firms with employees reporting to state employment security agencies, an increase of 2.4 percent over the previous year. Approximately 950,000 of these firms were new in 1995, and 840,000 firms no longer reported employees.

In our gaming model, the distribution of firm size depends not only on how fast firms—on average—expand or contract, but also on the rate at which new firms enter the economy. This has important implications for public policy.

It is the free entry of firms into the economic system that enables the economy to show the constant fixed employment size distribution of firms. When new firms enter the economy, they challenge existing firms, ensuring that the system remains dynamic.

A Summary of Major Statistical Findings

1. Large businesses (those with 500 or more employees) created all the 679,000 jobs in this 1989-91 recessionary period. In fact, these large businesses offset the job losses experienced by small business. Firms that remained small in both periods lost 192,000 workers. The number of workers in firms that remained large in both periods increased by 802,000. On net, small firms that became large and large firms that became small added 69,000 jobs.

2. The number of new firms with employees is a significant portion of total firms. The number of new firms that reported no employees in previous years is much higher than had earlier been reported. These new firms were practically all categorized as small business. Over the 1989-91 period, small companies accounted for 80 percent of all jobs lost. These job losses were attributable to firm layoffs and firms that went out of business. Thus, employment generated by small startup businesses was offset by employment losses in small busi-

nesses. Employment losses by large companies, in contrast, are 20 percent of the jobs lost by small firms.

Another way of saying this is that you are four times more likely to lose your job if you work for a small business than if you work for a large one. If you work for a small business, you will, on average, earn less than if you work for a large business, will have inferior or no retirement benefits, and will probably have no employer-provided health insurance. Virtually all workers in firms with 500 or more employees have employer-provided health insurance.

3. For the diverse economic periods 1982–87, 1989–91, and 1991–93, the number of firms with 5 or more workers has increased their employment was equal to the number of firms that decreased their employment. The size distribution of firms did not change in the decade, and there is evidence that it has not changed since the end of World War II. In the 1989-91 period, the number of firms that were large and became small equals the number that were small and became large.

4. The increases in employment in firms that became large were about equal to the decreases in employment of large firms that became small. Essentially, the employment shifts between small and large firms were mirror images of each other.

5. The distribution of employment by firm size is highly skewed. In 1991, just under 14,000 firms employed 45 percent of the private nonfarm workforce. The remaining 5 million firms employed the remaining 55 percent. This highly skewed distribution—a small number of large firms accounting for a highly disproportionate share of total em-

ployment—is observed in virtually all industries and in all free industrial countries. Obviously the same competitive forces are at work generating these similar distributions.

6. Given these competitive conditions, it is easy to show that simple statistical chance—what economists call *a random stochastic system*—is at work creating these distributions. A simple dynamic gaming model, previously proposed by several industrial economists, explains the inevitability of such a highly skewed concentration of jobs among a few large firms. Given the competitive nature of our economy, the resulting size distribution is predictable. For the first time, we have firm counts and employment data for the same firms over time that are used to test the model.

What You Can Do

At the beginning of this book, I stated that the issue of jobs is emotionally charged. This emotional impact—whether we are consciously aware of it or not—carries over into the political debate.

The political appointees at the SBA and the small business lobby well understand the power of the small business job-generation argument to help promote their political agenda. Their strategy is to tout—as loudly and as often as possible—the proposition that small business creates all the jobs.

Their mantra is simple and politically effective—but false. Yet the SBA's argument has been put forth in many areas: American working men and women should not be covered by mandated employer health insurance because this will greatly harm small businesses—*they create all the jobs*. The minimum wage should not be raised because it will hurt small businesses—*they create all the jobs.* Similar arguments mislead the public on environmental regulation, workplace safety, and business tax reduction.

The small business lobby has become the strongest advocacy institution in Congress and the White House. This lobby has distorted the job-generation issue and has assaulted the integrity of the federal/state statistical system. Most important, however, the SBA and its allies have sought to impose a policy of economic impoverishment on the American people.

The federal government's job-generation hoax is not an academic issue. No independent, responsible economist will argue that small business creates all the jobs and that therefore some policy prescription follows. Nor is the truth about job generation a result of perspective—of whether you call the glass half empty or half full. No responsible economist or statistician who has looked carefully at the data will support the SBA's position. Neither will you, if you have taken the time to examine the data.

Now that you have read this book, you can do something about the job-generation hoax. The next time a politician argues that small business creates all the jobs and that we must therefore adopt a particular course of action, you will be able to openly contradict his or her assertion. The information in this book will enable you to do so. And by doing so, you will be helping to restore integrity to the political debate.

Technical Appendices

The following appendices are provided for economists, systems analysts, and those wishing to examine the data in considerable detail.

For the first time, firm size employment and payroll data on the entire private nonfarm economy have been made available to the public. These data cover the period 1989–91, showing employment by firm size in 1989 and, for the same firms, employment by firm size in 1991. They enable interested researchers to examine the job-generation process in detail.

Because the Census Bureau data are generally unfamiliar to those outside that agency, Appendix A provides a detailed technical description. These data are based on payroll tax reports submitted by all businesses and no sampling error is involved.

Detailed tables developed from the Census Bureau data are provided in Appendix B to assist the reader in the analysis. Summary job-creation tables are provided for two employment-size groups, those firms with less than 500 workers and those with more than 500 workers. Job-generation statistics remain difficult for many economists to conceptualize. The rationale for the approach taken is discussed.

Comparable data are provided in Appendix C for firms with less than 5, 20, 50, and 100 employees.

A set of computer programming instructions is provided in Appendix D. Several federal agencies, universities, research organizations, and the 51 state employment security agencies have access to longitudinal firm data. Many have expressed interest in the job-creation process. If tabulations were prepared in a standard format, a library of information could be assembled and made available to assist future researchers.

Data for firms and establishments by size for the post–World War II period are provided in Appendix E. The distributions of establishment data from 1946–96 and firm data for 1982–87 and 1989–91 are discussed.

Appendix F provides a methodology for allocating boundary-crossers, firms that were small and became large and firms that were large and became small, between small and large firm employment job generation.

Appendix G provides the original Census Bureau statistics by major industry division. Five data items are proved for each cell: the number of firms, employment in 1989 and 1991, and the annual payroll in 1989 and 1991.

Appendix A

Sources of the Census Bureau Data

Employment data are collected quarterly from all private non-farm firms, as part of the payroll tax withholding system in the United States.

When a firm hires its first worker it must obtain an Employer Identification Number (EIN) from the Internal Revenue Service. The EIN is used by the federal government to keep track of payroll taxes (Social Security and withholding) and other taxes due from the firm. The application for an EIN provides data for industrial and geographic-location coding purposes. Each quarter all private nonfarm firms that are subject to income tax withholding or Social Security taxes must file a Form 941, Employer's Quarterly Federal Tax Return.

The EIN is used on all business tax forms.

For the first quarter report, the firm is also asked to report the number of workers on its payroll as of March 15. Under long-standing arrangements, the Bureau of the Census obtains these files from the IRS. By law the Census Bureau must maintain the confidentiality of these reports, and severe felony penalties can be imposed for any breach. These data, for the most part, are based on firm tax reports. To obtain detailed industry and county statistics, the annual Census Bureau Company Organization Survey of all large multi-establishment firms is conducted annually. The resulting file, along with other supplementary information, is referred to as the Standard Statistical Establishment List (SSEL).

Initially, the Office of Advocacy and the Census Bureau arranged to match the 1982–87 SSEL files, using a 2–percent sample to determine the size distribution of business firms and to determine the differential rate of growth between small and large firms. Sample data for years ending in 2 and 7 were available because these were the years the industrial censuses were taken. These tabulations at the regional and major-industry level provided statistics on the formation and termination of firms, by firm size, as well as the percentage employment growth and decline. Because of confidentiality, no employment data were provided.

Because of the different sampling methods used in the annual Census Bureau Company Organization Survey for industrial census years, the distributions of employment by firm size for 1982–87 and 1989–91 are not strictly comparable.

Under special arrangements a set of tables was specified that provided a matrix by employment size in 1989 and size in 1991, by major-industry division, for a national count of firms, employment in 1989 and 1991, as well as annual payrolls for both years. This was accomplished by matching both annual files by enterprise number. See Appendix D for additional details regarding the computer matching instructions. The annual files for 1989 and 1991 included all firms that reported some payroll either in 1989 or 1991. When a firm record in 1989 did not appear in 1991 it was classed as a firm exit (death). When a firm record in 1991 did not appear in 1989, it was classed as a firm entrant (birth). Note that the firm may have continued in business without having any workers in the March employment reporting period.

Firms may experience an EIN change because of a change in legal form of organization, mergers, acquisitions, reorganizations, and divestitures. The EIN keeps track of the payroll taxes owed and those legally obligated to pay them, and is not designed for the tracking of firms and employment over extended periods of time. The Census Bureau is currently undertaking an effort to improve the establishment matching, using address, industry, location, and other information. For additional information regarding the SSEL, see the United States Bureau of the Census' *The Standard Statistical Establishment List*, Technical Paper 44, 1979.

Appendix B

Supplementary Tables to Chapter 4: 1989–91 Data

Table B.1, the 1989–91 private nonfarm employment table of workers by firm size in 1989 and firm size in 1991, shows the dynamic employment changes in small and large firms, including births and deaths. As mentioned previously, the matrix data from the Census Bureau permits the counting of workers in firms for both periods that were small in 1989 and large in 1991, as well as firms that were large in 1989 and small in 1991.

Table B.1 needs some explanation. The table was created by matching two firm-employment files for 1989 and for 1991. Initially, both the 1989 and 1991 files were sorted and matched by the firm's Employer Identification Number (EIN), creating a single record containing the employment in 1989 and 1991. When matching two files by EIN, three possible match conditions exist.

The first match condition is that a firm (EIN) exists in the 1989 file but there is no matching firm (EIN) in the 1991 file. The firm by definition is classed as a "death" in that it reported no payroll in 1991. The second match condition is that a firm (EIN) exists in the 1991 file but there is no matching firm (EIN) in the 1989 file. The firm by definition is classed as a "birth" in that it reported no payroll in 1989. The third match condition occurs when a firm exists in both years. For each of these match conditions, a record is created which contains the employment for both 1989 and 1991. To simplify the sorting process, codes are assigned identifying the firm size in 1989 and in 1991, and identifying firm births and deaths.

These records from the matching process are then sorted by size in 1989 and 1991. The tabulation shows the employment in 1989 and 1991 for all possible size classes and the birth and death of firms. The rows provide the firm-size class in 1989 and the columns show the firm-size class in 1991. The top row of the table shows that there were 965,000 workers in firms with less than 5 employees in 1991 that did not exist in 1989. The left column reports that there were 1,192,000 workers in firms with less than 5 employees in 1989 who no longer had employees in 1991 because the firms might have gone out of business, continued operations without employees, or changed their legal form of ownership and thus their EIN. The bottom right shows 39,463,000 workers in large firms (500 or more employees) in 1989 and 40,455,000 workers in these same firms that remained large in 1991.

If one wants the total of workers in 1989 (91,626,000), all the rows for 1989 for all size groups must be added. If one

Table B.1

Employment in Private Nonfarm Firms by Firm Size, 1989 and 1991 (in thousands)

Size of firm in 1989	Not active in 1991	Employment size in 1991					
		0-4	5-19	20-49	50-99	100-499	500 +
Not active in 1989							
1989 employment	0	0	0	0	0	0	0
1991 employment	0	965	1,696	1,195	904	1,606	1,472
0-4 employees							
1989 employment	1,192	3,202	645	13	2	1	>0.5
1991 employment	0	3,512	2,126	525	242	242	66
5-19 employees							
1989 employment	2,247	1,568	8,776	938	36	7	>0.5
1991 employment	0	655	8,813	1,642	188	93	26
20-49 employees							
1989 employment	1,632	225	1,563	5,863	829	61	1
1991 employment	0	15	880	5,895	1,308	250	28

50-99 employees							
1989 employment	1,201	94	198	1,197	3,732	754	4
1991 employment	0	2	37	759	3,753	1,225	49
100-499 employees							
1989 employment	2,062	96	140	256	1,098	9,098	623
1991 employment	0	1	9	61	669	9,266	1,208
500 + employees							
1989 employment	1,662	35	50	76	82	904	39,463
1991 employment	0	>0.5	>0.5	2	4	461	40,455

Source: United States Census Bureau, Standard Statistical Establishment List match.

wants the total of workers in 1991 (92,305,000), all the columns for 1991 for all size groups must be added.

It is virtually impossible to visually understand these data without simplifying their presentation. To make the data easier to understand we created Table B.2, which does two things: It provides marginal totals, that is, row and column sums. In addition, it summarizes the five smallest-size classes into a 0–499 firm class. Note that a firm that came into existence in 1989, but after March, will have zero employees and be classed in the 0–4 employment category.

Table B.2 also requires some additional comment so that the information is understandable. Permit a personal note. I have worked with employment statistics for almost 40 years. In spite of my experience it was months before it became obvious what the data were conveying. It was even more difficult to understand the economic process at work that would provide an explanation of the forces that generated these statistical results. Remember that we are not used to viewing employment data presented in this way.

In total, only 12 numbers are involved: small to small (2); large to large (2); small to large (2); large to small (2); births of small and large (2); and deaths of small and large (2), aside from row or column totals. The complexity in presenting these statistics is created by the fact that firms that change their size status cannot easily be characterized in the table. The reason for this descriptive complexity is that employment size in 1989 and 1991 changes, and one must keep track of net and gross effects, while at the same time observing changes that occur in firm-size status from one period to the next. Essentially, the table is multidimensional, providing information by year, by firm size and status (births and deaths), by employ-

Table B.2

Employment by Firm Size, 1989 and 1991 (in thousands)

	Active in 1989 or 1991	Not in 1991 (deaths)	Employment in 1991	
			0–499	500 +
Row 1				
Active in 1989 and/or 1991				
1989 employment	91,626	9,996		
1991 employment	92,305		49,001	43,304
Net	679			
Row 2 (births)				
Not active in 1989				
1989 employment				
1991 employment	7,838		6,366	1,472
Row 3				
0-499 employees				
1989 employment	49,354	8,334	40,392	628
1991 employment		42,168	1,377	
Net	−5,809	−8,334	1,776	749
Row 4				
500+ employees				
1989 employment	42,272	1,662	1,147	39,463
1991 employment			467	40,455
Net	−1,450	−1,662	−680	992

Sources: Special tabulation from the Census Bureau Standard Statistical Establishment List files summarized from Appendix G, Table G.1.

ment in the initial period, and by employment in the final period.

It is important to note that when a firm moves from a small-size class (less than 500 workers) to a large-size class, one cannot easily characterize the firm's status in a table. The issue is best understood using a worker migration analogy—keeping track of worker migration between regions. Substitute "region 1" for firm size 0–4. To analyze what is happening in this region during the period, one would try to learn what has occurred as the result of labor force entrants, retirees, and the sum of in-migrants less out-migrants. To obtain a net migration statistic, workers who were in other regions in 1989 who came into region 1 in 1991 have to be added, while those who worked in region 1 in 1989 and left have to be subtracted. This is what must be done to analyze what is occurring for a specific employment-size class.

In reality, however, instead of "region 1," "small business" is substituted to carry out the arithmetic. Tabulating the data in this way answers the question, "How many jobs were created in this two-year period by small and large firms?"

The problem here is unique. It is important to note that the characteristic of the observation is changing, and as a result we need to be more precise in what we characterize as small or large. Assume that a worker in a rural area in year 1 moves to an urban area in year 2 and that the worker experiences an increase of hourly earnings from $6 per hour to $10 per hour. There is no argument that the worker has gained $4. However, it would be a mistake to attribute this $4 gain solely to the rural area or the urban area. In the same way it is necessary to be precise and state how many jobs were created by small firms that became large, and how many were lost by large firms that became small.

A treasure-trove of information is shown in Table B.2. For the first time one can analyze what has happened to private nonfarm employment by employment firm size and status for the same firms in two periods, 1989 and 1991. By summing the appropriate rows, one can determine how many workers were employed in 1989 (91,626,000). By summing the appropriate columns, one can determine how many workers were employed in 1991 (92,305,000). Thus employment grew by 679,000.

Total employment in 1989 comprises employment in small and large firms. The number employed in 1989 is made up of three components for the two size groups in 1991. The small-firm employment for 1989 is made up of small firms that died in 1991, employment in firms that remained small in both periods, plus employment in small firms that became large in 1991.

The large-firm employment for 1989 is made up of large firms that died in 1991, firms that remained large in both periods, plus employment in large firms that became small in 1991.

For 1991, employment in small and large firms is defined in a similar fashion, by their size status and birth status in 1989.

In Table B.2, the first column and row define firm status in 1989 and 1991 and provide a count of employment by size of firm in both years.

The first data column in Table B.2 also provides an employment count in 1989 by size of firm in 1989. The second data column provides employment in 1991 by size of firm in 1991. Employment by firm size in both periods is displayed.

For 1989, Table B.2 shows how many employees there were in small firms in 1989 and their firm-size status in 1991. Specifically, Row 3 shows how many were employed in small firms in 1989. These include the number of workers employed in firms that were no longer in business in 1991; the workers employed in firms that were small in both periods; and the number of workers employed in firms that were small in 1989 and became large in 1991.

Row 4 shows how many were employed in large firms in 1989. These include the number of workers employed in firms that were no longer in business in 1991; the number of workers employed in firms that were large in 1989 and became small in 1991; and the workers employed in firms that were large in both periods.

In summary, births and deaths of small and large firms are shown in the second and third columns and the rows for small and large firms. Also shown are employment statistics for those firms that were small in 1989 and large in 1991, as well as for those that were large in 1989 and small in 1991.

The first data column in Table B.2 provides employment in 1989 by size of firm in 1989. It shows 91,626,000 workers in 1989, with 49,354,000 employed in small firms. The second data row in Row 1 provides employment in 1991 by size of firm in 1991. It shows 92,305,000 workers in 1991, with 49,001,000 employed in small firms. As noted previously, 353,000 fewer workers were employed in small businesses in 1991, but there were 1,032,000 more workers in large firms.

In 1989 there were 8,366,000 workers in small firms that did not exist in 1991. In 1991 there were 6,366,000 workers in small firms that had not existed in 1989.

The bottom right portion of the table shows employment in 1989 and 1991 for those firms that were small in both periods and for those firms that were large in both periods. In 1989 there were 40,392,000 workers in firms that were small in both 1989 and 1991, and in 1991 there were 42,168,000 in firms that were small in both 1989 and 1991. Employment in firms that were small in both periods increased by 1,776,000; employment in firms that were large in both periods increased by 992,000.

The off diagonal elements (/) are also shown, providing employment statistics for those that worked in small firms in 1989 and in large firms in 1991, as well as for those that worked in large firms in 1989 and in small firms in 1991.

These four numbers are at the heart of the job-generation problem: Employment in firms that were large in 1989 and small in 1991 declined from 1,147,000 to 467,000. Employment in firms that were small in 1989 and large in 1991 increased from 628,000 to 1,377,000. Note that these employees that shifted from small to large firms, and from large to small firms, are carefully labeled. These elements have confused the methodological debate. These flows are offsetting. On net, 69,000 more workers went from small to large (749,000) than went from large to small (680,000).

Appendix C

Job-Generation Statistics for Firms with Fewer than 5, 20, 50, and 100 Workers

For purposes of exposition, the SBA's Office of Advocacy's definition of a small business, a firm with less than 500 employees, has been used in the analysis. Intuitively, this figure seems too high. For example, several large drug companies in *Fortune*'s list of major industry firms employ less than 500 workers. Given the availability of Census Bureau data, we are not restricted to this measure. Analytical tables can readily be prepared for firms by size class in 1989 and 1991.

It is quite useful to note that for all small firms, those with less than 5, 20, 50, and 100 workers, the job generators were not small businesses. In no instance did they create more than a small fraction of the 681,000 jobs generated by the total private nonfarm economy.

As Table C.1 indicates, those businesses that were small, with less than 5 workers, and remained small generated only 83,000 jobs during the 1989–91 period. Those that were large and remained large generated 1,332,000 jobs. On net, those that were small and became large and those that were large and became small lost 734,000 jobs. It is important to observe that if this net loss of 734,000 jobs were to be attributed to large businesses, the large business sector would still have generated the vast majority of jobs.

The same observations may be made for firms with less than 20 employees, as shown in Table C.2, and for firms with less than 50 employees, as shown in Table C.3.

The picture is even clearer for those firms with less than 100 workers as revealed in Table C.4. It was the large firms, those with 100 or more workers, that created all the jobs and made up for the job losses in small firms.

Table C.1

Nonfarm Firm Employment in 1989–1991, by Size of Firm in 1989 and 1991 (Small: < 5 employees; Large: 5 employees or more)

Firm Size Status		Employment		
1989	1991	1989	1991	Net
Small	Small	4,394,000	4,477,000	83,000
Large	Large	75,750,000	77,083,000	1,332,000
Small	Large	661,000	10,074,000	9,414,000
Large	Small	10,821,000	674,000	148,000
Sum of small to large and large to small				−734,000
	Total	91,626,000	92,308,000	681,000

Source: Census Bureau tabulations. See Appendix G, Table G.1.
Note: Calculations are based on unrounded data.

Table C.2

Nonfarm Firm Employment in 1989–1991, by Size of Firm in 1989 and 1991 (Small: < 20 employees; Large: 20 employees or more)

Firm Size Status		Employment		
1989	1991	1989	1991	Net
Small	Small	17,630,000	17,768,000	137,000
Large	Large	55,759,000	57,090,000	1,331,000
Small	Large	997,000	8,202,000	7,205,000
Large	Small	8,957,000	945,000	−8,012,000
Sum of small to large and large to small				−807,000
	Total	91,626,000	92,308,000	681,000

Source: Census Bureau tabulations. See Appendix G, Table G.1.
Note: Calculations are based on unrounded data.

Table C.3

Nonfarm Firm Employment in 1989–1991, by Size of Firm in 1989 and 1991 (Small: < 50 employees; Large: 50 employees or more)

Firm Size Status		Employment		
1989	1991	1989	1991	Net
Small	Small	27,863,000	27,919,000	56,000
Large	Large	55,759,000	57,090,000	1,331,000
Small	Large	937,000	6,426,000	5,489,000
Large	Small	7,067,000	872,000	−6,195,000
Sum of small to large and large to small				−706,000
	Total	91,626,000	92,308,000	681,000

Source: Census Bureau tabulations. See Appendix G, Table G.1.
Note: Calculations are based on unrounded data.

Table C.4

Nonfarm Firm Employment in 1989–1991, by Size of Firm in 1989 and 1991 (Small: <100 employees; Large: 100 employees or more)

Firm Size Status		Employment		
1989	1991	1989	1991	Net
Small	Small	35,152,000	35,113,000	−38,000
Large	Large	50,088,000	52,391,000	1,303,000
Small	Large	828,000	5,058,000	4,230,000
Large	Small	5,558,000	746,000	−4,813,000
Sum of small to large and large to small				−583,000
	Total	91,626,000	92,308,000	681,000

Source: Census Bureau tabulations. See Appendix G, Table G.1.
Note: Calculations are based on unrounded data.

Appendix D
Computer Processing Instructions

Several federal agencies, universities, research organizations, and the fifty-one state employment security agencies have access to longitudinal firm data. Many have expressed interest in the job-creation process. If tabulations were prepared in a standard format, a library of information could be assembled and made available to assist future researchers.

The following is an outline of the computer programs necessary to carry out additional job-generation studies from quarterly payroll establishment reports. The instructions below outline the necessary steps.

Step 1:

1. Summarize the quarterly payroll data into one record. Use the March monthly employment figure for the year. The federal data has only the March employment data and the aim

is to generate comparable statistics across states and industries. Combine the establishment data into one record for the firm. One wants to select the industry of the largest establishment in the case of multiple Standard Industrial Classification codes (SICs), add up the employment and payroll for the year, and be able to match each firm's report with another's year report.

2. Sort the file by firm, by establishment, by county, and by industry. If a main frame computer is used, set the output file so that its firm identification codes and industry and geographic codes will be written in the same format as the single establishment firm records.

3. Select the largest establishment's industry and geographic codes. When the first record is read in, move the firm codes to the output area, add in the employment and payroll, and move the employment to a "test" area.

4. Read in the next record and test to determine if the firm is new. If it is new, write the record in memory. If it is not new, add the employment and payroll. If the current record's employment is larger than the test area employment, move in the new industry and area codes, and move in the new employment to the test area. In this way, the establishment with the largest employment will have its industry and area codes assigned, and the employment and payroll totaled.

Step 2. Repeat this process for each annual file.

Step 3. Match two annual files by firm number, creating one output file. Three match file conditions are possible: both files match; there is a record in the early file, but not in the later file; there is a record in the later file, but not in the early file.

Each firm record in the resulting matched output file should have the following information:

1. State and/or federal EIN code.
2. Early year, major industry division code.
3. Later year, major industry division code.
4. Early year employment size code.
5. Later year employment size code.
6. Early SIC.
7. Later SIC.
8. Early employment, blank if no report.
9. Later employment, blank if no report.
10. Early payroll, blank if no report.
11. Later payroll, blank if no report.
12. Early county or SMSA codes.
13. Later county or SMSA codes.

Items 12 and 13 are needed if the state wants additional runs for its areas.

Each record in the resulting file now has an SIC code for at least one year. If no SIC code for the early year, assign the later-year code. If the SIC for the early year differs from that of the later year, use the later SIC. The assumption is that the later code is better and more accurate than the early SIC code.

The proposed major-industry division codes and firm employment size codes are shown below.

SIC	Major Industry Division	Code
07–09	Agriculture, forestry, and fisheries	1
10–14	Mining	2

SIC	Major Industry Division	Code
15–17	Construction	3
20–39	Manufacturing	4
40–49	Transportation, communications, and utilities	5
50–51	Wholesale trade	6
52–59	Retail trade	7
60–67	Finance, insurance, and real estate	8
70–99	Services	9

Employment Size Codes

Employment	Code
No report	0
0–4	1
5–19	2
20–49	3
50–99	4
100–499	5
500 or more	6

Step 4. Sort the file by industry (SIC), by employment size codes in early and later years.

Step 5. Tabulate the file by SIC, by size in early year, by size in later year, summing the firm counts and adding the employment and payrolls. Note that the employment and payroll totals should check against state totals, but the industry totals will differ because of the firm summary process and the SIC over-the-year code changes.

Appendix E

The Size Distribution of Establishments and Firms in the Post–World War II Period

Part A—1946 to Date, Establishment Data

Since the end of World War II, the size distribution of establishments has been remarkably stable, as seen in Table E.1. Note that an establishment is not a firm. A firm can own several establishments, and a large firm may have many small establishments. Because businesses by size are being studied, firm data are more useful, but there are no comprehensive data for firms until 1982.

What was happening to the size distribution of firms, as

opposed to establishments, during this 50-year postwar period? Because of the way the government compiles its data, there is no definitive way to answer that question. There are no consistent long-term historical data on the size distribution of employment by firm size. Business income tax forms do not request an employment statistic. However, the Census Bureau, as part of its County Business Pattern (CBP) program, has provided a special tabulation of the number of establishments by five establishment employment-size classes for the 1946–96 period. The data are shown in Table E.1.

Unfortunately, these data are not comparable for various periods. Prior to 1974 all the data collected for a firm's establishments in a county were combined into one report. Beginning in 1974, establishments of the same company in the same county were no longer combined. Prior to 1983, only establishments that had employees in the fourth quarter were counted. Beginning with 1983, establishments with employees in any quarter were counted. Beginning in 1984, coverage was extended to a large number of nonprofit organizations. In general, CBP data currently reflect all private nonfarm employees covered by Social Security.

The data are not comparable over extended periods. However, assuming that no significant structural changes in the distribution occurred during those years when the data are not comparable, the series reveals that there has been no change in the employment-size distribution of establishments for over 50 years.

Since 1984, when the establishment data were first compiled and published on a consistent basis, there has been virtually no change in the size distribution of establishments as measured by employment class.

Table E.1

Total Establishments and Distribution of Establishments by Employment Size, 1946–1992

Year	Number of establishments (in thousands) Total	Employment size class (in percent)				
		< 20	20-49	50-99	100-499	500 or more
1946	2,254	90.51	5.72	1.96	1.53	0.28
1948	2,675	90.86	5.55	1.88	1.43	0.28
1951	2,886	90.76	5.58	1.91	1.49	0.26
1953	2,940	90.67	5.64	1.96	1.46	0.28
1956	3,129	90.81	5.61	1.93	1.40	0.25
1959	3,303	90.84	5.65	1.86	1.40	0.24
1962	3,348	90.41	5.94	1.94	1.45	0.25
1964	3,458	90.15	6.11	2.00	1.49	0.25
1965	3,522	89.86	6.25	2.09	1.54	0.26
1966	3,542	89.29	6.59	2.19	1.64	0.29
1967	3,511	88.79	6.86	2.31	1.74	0.30
1968	3,503	88.27	7.19	2.41	1.81	0.31
1969	3,534	87.85	7.51	2.46	1.86	0.33
1970	3,521	87.43	7.74	2.56	1.94	0.33
1971	3,511	87.56	7.71	2.52	1.90	0.32
1972	3,541	87.00	8.10	2.60	1.97	0.33
1973	3,653	86.74	8.17	2.70	2.06	0.33
1974	4,110	87.90	7.52	2.50	1.78	0.29
1975	4,114	88.39	7.28	2.39	1.67	0.27

1976	4,143	88.07	7.43	2.49	1.74	0.27
1977	4,352	88.06	7.45	2.50	1.73	0.27
1978	4,409	87.07	8.05	2.73	1.87	0.28
1979	4,536	86.63	8.28	2.85	1.95	0.29
1980	4,543	86.55	8.29	2.89	2.00	0.28
1981	4,587	86.60	8.41	2.85	2.00	0.28
1982	4,634	86.61	8.39	2.84	1.95	0.27
1983	5,307	88.30	7.84	2.49	1.65	0.23
1984	5,518	87.88	7.54	2.60	1.74	0.23
1985	5,701	87.71	7.62	2.65	1.79	0.23
1986	5,807	87.51	7.73	2.69	1.84	0.23
1987	5,937	87.35	7.84	2.74	1.84	0.23
1988	6,019	87.17	7.93	2.78	1.88	0.24
1989	6,107	86.87	8.12	2.82	1.95	0.25
1990	6,176	86.70	8.24	2.84	1.98	0.24
1991	6,201	86.96	8.12	2.75	1.92	0.23
1992	6,318	87.16	8.02	2.71	1.87	0.24
1993	6,403	87.10	8.02	2.72	1.92	0.24
1994	6,509	86.98	8.09	2.73	1.96	0.25
1995	6,613	86.69	8.23	2.80	2.03	0.25
1996	6,738	86.70	8.19	2.81	2.05	0.25

Part B—Census Bureau Firm Formation Rates, 1982–91

For some time now the SBA's Office of Advocacy has had Census Bureau tabulations of firms by size that indicated how many were adding or losing workers. Because these data for 1982–87 were based on a 2-percent sample, the detailed industry data had too few observations in specific cells. Confidentiality rules did not permit the release of employment tabulations.

It is instructive to examine the data in some detail because of what we can learn about the real source of job generation in the United States. We can analyze which firms added or lost jobs by their employment size in both the 1982–87 and 1989–91 periods.

At the end of every calendar quarter, all business firms must report their payrolls and tax withholding for their employees to the Internal Revenue Service. In March the report requires the reporting of employment. The Census Bureau obtains these quarterly records from the IRS for statistical purposes. The file, referred to as the Standard Statistical Establishment List, is described in some detail in Appendix A.

Census Bureau Firm Count Data, 1982–87

By matching firms that existed in either 1982 or 1987, as specified, the Census Bureau tabulation provided counts of firms that increased, decreased, or remained unchanged during the period. In addition, the number of firms, as well as total employment and payrolls, was tallied by size of firm in 1989 and 1991—that is, by its size in 1989 cross-classified by its size in 1991. The 1982–87 firm data were tabulated using different specifications from the 1989–91 tabulations, so that the employment data could be made available and Census Bureau confidentiality could be maintained. This is not the usual way federal and state statistical agencies publish employment data.

The Census Bureau's firm-size tabulations for recent periods throw important light on the job-generation issue. Tables E.2 and E.3 report the number of firms by employment size for selected years from 1982 through 1991.

The Census Bureau maintains a historical 2-percent sample file of firms for the industrial census years—that is, every 5 years, for years ending in 2 and 7. Because the same sampling number pattern, based on the IRS's Employer Identification Number, was used for both periods, the same firms could be matched for both pairs of years.

These preliminary sample results were intriguing. They were preliminary in the sense that they were based on a small sample, and there was a need to develop a strategy to solve the confidentiality problem with regard to the employment data. The Census Bureau would not provide employment data for a cell if there were one or a small number of firms in a table entry. More than a few cases were required, so that those outside the Census Bureau could study them and the Census Bureau could be assured that the data were confidential (no outsider could identify a firm's employment).

I designed the 1989–91 tabulation to study what the job-generation rates would be if one examined the data either from the start or the end period. To meet this requirement, the data had to be tabulated in "matrix" form. Because this format

Table E.2

Number of Firms by Employment Size for Selected Years

Firm size	Employment		Percent distribution	
	1982*	1987*	1982	1987
Total	4,364,250	4,893,000	100.0	100.0
Zero	585,150	640,900	13.4	13.1
1–4	2,118,600	2,345,150	48.5	47.9
5–19	1,231,050	1,427,300	28.2	29.2
20–99	358,600	403,600	8.2	8.2
100–499	57,850	63,150	1.3	1.3
500 or more	13,000	13,500	0.3	0.3

*Based on a 2-percent random sample.

is not the usual way tabulations are presented, the general reader lacks a frame of reference to understand these statistics.

As shown in Table E.2, the size distribution of firms with employees in 1982 was almost identical to the size distribution in 1987, although the economy had expanded at a very rapid rate following the recovery from the 1980–81 recession.

For the two-year recessionary period, 1989–91, the size distribution of firms was also basically unchanged, as shown in Table E.3.

Because the basic Census Bureau data obtained from the IRS are edited differently in industrial census years—that is, in years ending in 2 and 7—the distributions for the 1982–87 period are not strictly comparable to those of the 1989–91 period.

Using the 2-percent sample of firms, the Census Bureau was asked to tabulate the distribution of firms by employment size in 1982 and provide a count of firms that increased or decreased over this period.

Table E.3

Number of Firms by Employment Size for 1989 and 1991

Firm size	Employment		Percent	
	1989	1991	1989	1991
Total	5,021,315	5,051,025	100.0	100.0
0–4	3,003,224	3,063,304	59.8	60.1
5–19	1,490,651	1,492,595	29.7	29.6
20–49	339,008	336,376	6.7	6.7
50–99	104,951	103,435	2.1	2.0
100–499	69,608	63,338	1.4	1.3
500 or more	13,873	13,977	0.3	0.3

Source: United States Bureau of the Census, special tabulations.

Table E.4

Percentage Distribution of Firms with Payrolls in Both 1982 and 1987 That Gained or Lost Employees, by Employment-Size Class

Employment firm size 1982	Firms with employment gains (in percent)	Firms with employment losses (in percent)
Zero employees*	84.6	0.0
1–4	36.8	21.7
5–19	44.7	43.4
20–99	50.0	46.8
100–499	47.6	51.6
500 or more	50.3	49.2

Source: United States Bureau of the Census, special tabulations.
*A zero-employee firm had some payroll in both 1982 and 1987.

Table E.4 shows the percentage distribution of firms with payrolls in both 1982 and 1987 that either had employment growth or employment losses.

These data uncovered unexpected insights. In the 1982–87 period, the probability that a firm would add employees to its payroll was equal to the probability that a firm would lose employees, if the firm employed more than 4 workers in 1982. Note that in this tabulation a zero-employee firm had some payroll in both 1982 and 1987. By definition it would not be included if it had no payroll in both 1982 and 1987. Some months later, the Office of Advocacy received the 1989–91 tabulations. The statistics for the 1989–91 period are shown in Table E.5.

The 1989–91 Census Bureau data revealed how the regression fallacy distorts the job-generation issue. Table E.6, shows the employment in 1989 and 1991 for firms that were in one size class in 1989 and in one higher or lower size (adjacent) class in 1991. Because the data originally were in matrix form for the 1989–91 period, for those firms that remained in the same employment-size class in both periods, one cannot determine how many increased, decreased, or maintained their employment.

However, it appears to be the case that in this period the same number of firms showed an increase in employment as showed a decrease in employment, because the employment distributions in both years are virtually the same. Moreover, the matrix-type tables tell us for those firms that moved to a different size group how many moved to a larger size group and how many moved to a smaller size group.

Just as reported for the 1982–87 period, the numbers in 1989–91, are about equal in both directions. Of those firms that crossed employment-size boundaries, we can see that about the same number of firms shifted to a higher size class as to a lower size class. The movements of firms across size boundaries are mirror images of each other.

One of the most interesting findings from the Census Bureau data is that the probability that a firm with more than 4

Table E.5

Number of Firms by Employment Firm Size in 1989 Cross-Classified by Firm Size in 1991

Firm size in 1989

	Not active in 1991	Firm size in 1991					
		0-4	5-19	20-49	50-99	100-499	500 or more
Not active in 1989		975,560	188,270	37,820	13,115	9,410	885
0-4	871,345	1,806,640	299,725	18,015	3,960	1,250	55
5-19	248,040	237,765	938,720	65,990	3,515	980	15
20-49	53,665	7,570	60,485	192,300	21,285	1,400	25
50-99	17,690	1,875	3,146	19,515	51,605	8,675	180
100-499	11,225	470	795	1,850	8,230	45,580	1,730
500 or more	1,480	70	45	35	55	1,360	11,265

Source: Census Bureau, Standard Statistical Establishment List match.

119

Table E.6

Firms Active in 1989 and 1991 That Were in One Size Class in 1989 and in One Higher or Lower Size Class in 1991

Size class			Size class		
1989	1991	Number of firms	1989	1991	Number of firms
2	1	237,765	1	2	299,725
3	2	60,485	2	3	65,990
4	3	19,515	3	4	21,285
5	4	8,230	4	5	8,675
6	5	1,360	5	6	1,730

Source: Census Bureau, special tabulations.

workers will add workers in the next period is equal to the probability that a firm will lay off workers.

This finding confirms Gibrat's law of proportional effect. That is, consider firms with employment in two periods, classified by their initial size. In all the size groups with more than 4 workers, the same number of firms existing in both periods increased their employment as decreased their employment. This was true for the 1982–87 period and the 1989–91 period.

The earlier tabulations, 1982–87, showed counts of firm employment changes only. No tallies of employment were provided because of confidentiality considerations on the part of the Census Bureau. The 1989–91 tabulation, in addition, included a cross tabulation of size of firm in 1989 (six employment-size classes) and size of firm in 1991. Also, total employment and total payrolls were reported for the 48 six-size classes, including 6 for births and 6 for deaths. For firm "births," the number of firms, total employment, and payrolls were tallied by size of firm in 1991. For firm "deaths," the number of firms, total employment, and payrolls were tallied by size of firm in 1989. Detailed data by major-industry division are provided in Appendix G.

Because the data are in matrix form in the 1989–91 period, one cannot determine how many firms that remained in the same employment size class in both periods increased and how many decreased. Although we do not know how many added or lost workers, we do know the net employment change if they remained in the same employment category in both periods.

The matrix table tells us how many firms and how many workers moved to larger size classes and how many moved to smaller size classes. Again, the finding is that the numbers are about equal in both directions. Moreover, the firm-size distributions are unchanged. This result conforms to our earlier finding that the employment establishment size has been unchanged.

In summary, previous Census Bureau tabulations for 1982 and 1987 showed that for firms with employment of 5 or more, irrespective of size in 1982, the probability of increasing their employment was equal to the probability of decreasing their employment in 1987. That is, the same number of firms gained employment as lost employment. This is not true of the smallest size class because the size class is bounded by zero. Therefore, if a firm with 1 or 2 employees lost 1 or 2 workers it would be classed as a death.

In 1991, there were about 1.2 million new firms in the system. "New" here is defined as having no employment in

1989. These firms have more volatile employment changes because they might be in an expansion phase or operating according to more long-term decision considerations than other larger and established firms.

What these statistics suggest is an economic world where firms add or lose employment on a random basis, without regard to their initial size. The exceptions are the newest and smallest firms. Whether those firms that experienced employment growth after growing in the initial period continued to do so in subsequent periods is a research question the Census Bureau data can answer as more comparable annual files become available. The effect of changing economic activity on these probabilities by firm size would also add to our knowledge of job creation.

The original Census Bureau tabulations provide six size classes: 0–4 (size 1), 5–19 (size 2), 20–49 (size 3), 50–99 (size 4), 100–499 (size 5), and 500 or more (size 6). The off-diagonal adjacent elements (for example, those firms in size 2 in 1989 and in size 1 in 1991) are similar to those in the opposite off-diagonal adjacent position (i.e., those in size 1 in 1989 and in size 2 in 1991). This is true for both the number of firms and employment.

Table E.6 shows that (except for the smallest-size-class changers, 1 to 2 and 2 to 1) the number of firms that moved from one off-diagonal adjacent size class in the initial period to one larger size class was about equal to the number of firms that moved from one off-diagonal adjacent size class in the initial period to one smaller size class. An upward trend is evident, but it should be noted that if the 1,230,000 firm deaths are considered boundary crossers, the overwhelming number of 1989 existing firms lost employees.

Labor Department Statistics Annual Rates of Firm Births and Deaths, 1982–95

The stability of the size distribution of firms is in contrast with firm volatility—the births and deaths of firms. New data from the U.S. Department of Labor's Employment and Training Administration provide a count of the births and deaths of firms covered by state unemployment compensation laws. These data indicate that birth and death rates are much higher than previously reported.

During the 1982–95 period, firm-formation rates (births) averaged 17 percent per year, but were considerably lower during the 1990–92 recession period. Firm-termination rates (deaths) were 15 percent.

In my October 1994 article, "On the Formation of Business Firms," published in the U.S. Department of Labor's Monthly Labor Review, I reported on firm-formation and firm-termination rates. The original data were obtained from state employment security agencies that report to the U.S. Department of Labor's Employment and Training Administration.

The series starts in 1982. The number of firms over the 13 years for which there is data has grown by 2 percent a year, or about the same rate of growth as that of the work force. However, the net growth rate masks the volatility of the firm-formation process. Gross rates for new firm formation averaged 16 percent and net termination rates averaged 14 percent since 1982.

The firm-formation numbers involved are a measure of economic activity. At the beginning of 1995, there were

Table E.7

The Number of U.S. Firms and the Components of Firm Change, 1982–1996

Year	Successor firms	New firms sum	New and successors	Terminations	Firms at end of year
1982	185,199	595,819	781,018	706,594	4,743,844
1983	171,207	632,922	804,129	716,925	4,831,048
1984	164,075	690,812	854,887	685,585	5,000,350
1985	166,337	714,522	880,859	754,083	5,127,126
1986	175,242	724,520	899,762	814,161	5,212,727
1987	163,182	748,274	911,456	730,845	5,393,338
1988	153,066	733,021	886,087	769,513	5,509,912
1989	153,027	744,654	897,681	837,186	5,570,407
1990	146,021	769,124	915,145	844,053	5,641,499
1991	136,816	727,497	864,313	820,538	5,685,274
1992	137,864	736,773	874,637	819,336	5,740,575
1993	135,627	775,746	911,373	800,660	5,851,288
1994	134,861	793,848	928,709	793,142	5,986,855
1995	163,245	819,477	982,722	865,352	6,104,225
1996	175,625	842,357	1,017,982	850,508	6,271,699

Components of annual change (in percent)

Year	Successor firms	New firms sum	New and successors	Terminations	Firms at end of year
1982	3.90	12.56	16.46	14.89	1.57
1983	3.54	13.10	16.65	14.84	1.81
1984	3.28	13.82	17.10	13.71	3.39
1985	3.24	13.94	17.18	14.71	2.47

Components of annual change—selected years (in percent)

Period					
1986	3.36	13.90	17.26	15.62	1.64
1987	3.03	13.87	16.90	13.55	3.35
1988	2.78	13.30	16.08	13.97	2.12
1989	2.75	13.37	16.12	15.03	1.09
1990	2.59	13.63	16.22	14.96	1.26
1991	2.41	12.80	15.20	14.43	0.77
1992	2.40	12.83	15.24	14.27	0.96
1993	2.32	13.26	15.58	13.68	1.89
1994	2.25	13.26	15.51	13.25	2.26
1995	2.67	13.42	16.10	14.18	1.92
1996	2.80	13.43	16.23	13.56	2.67
AVG 1982–96	2.89	13.37	16.25	14.31	1.94
AVG 1982–86	3.47	13.46	16.93	14.75	2.17
AVG 1987–91	2.71	13.40	16.10	14.39	1.72
AVG 1992–96	2.49	13.24	15.73	13.79	1.94

Source: State employment security agency quarterly reports to the U.S. Department of Labor, Employment and Training Administration.

more than 6 million firms with employees reporting to state employment security agencies, an increase of 2.4 percent over the previous year; about 950,000 were new in that year; and 840,000 firms no longer reported employees.

Appendix F

Allocating Boundary-Crosser Employment

Although the Small Business Administration (SBA) has created a great deal of confusion in the measurement of crossover firms—firms that were small and became large and firms that were large and became small—a simple solution to the problem was suggested by Dwight French, a statistician at the Department of Energy's Information Agency (EIA).

Assume a cutoff of firms with less than 500 employees to be small and firms with 500 or more employees to be large. When a firm goes from 400 workers to 600, according to the SBA, this small business generated 200 jobs. The SBA attributes this 200-employee increase to the small firm group because that was the firm's initial status. When that same firm falls back to 400, the 200 lost jobs are attributed to the large firm group because that was the firm's initial status that year. Obviously this methodology is not only biased, it makes no sense.

A better counting rule that is consistent with our definition of small and large firms should be adopted by those examining the job-generation issue.

When our example firm started with 400 workers and added 200 workers, it added 100 workers as a small firm. It then became a large firm. When it added the next 100 workers, it added them as a large firm. Conversely, when the firm lost 200 workers, the same counting rule should apply. That is, when it lost the first 100 workers, it did so as a large firm. When it lost the next 100 workers, it did so as a small firm.

Before turning to the actual Census Bureau data, let us examine another example. A firm with 40 employees increases to 510 employees in the next period. I propose to count this 470-employee increase in the following manner: The first 460 jobs should be counted in the small-business column. Only the next 10 jobs should be allocated to the large-business sector.

Because the 1989–91 Census Bureau data are in matrix form, as shown in Table G.1, the data are readily available and the calculations are simple. On net, boundary-crossers created 70,250 jobs.

To understand how this number was derived, first focus on firms that went from small to large. The Census Bureau reported 1,842 firms that were small in 1989 and large in 1991. In 1989 those firms employed 627,987 workers. In 1991 they employed 1,378,009 workers. This was a gain of 750,022.

At some point between 1989 and 1991, these 1,842 firms,

while still small, employed, at a maximum, 921,000 workers as small firms. That is, 1,842 multiplied by 500 equals 921,000. Thus, while these firms were small they added 293,013 workers—that is, 921,000 less 627,987 equals 293,013. Firms that became large by passing the 499 mark added 457,009. That is, 750,022 less 293,013 equals 457,009.

Now let us focus on firms that went from large to small. The Census Bureau reported 1,842 firms that were large in 1989 and small in 1991. In 1989 they employed 1,147,159 workers. In 1991 they employed 467,387 workers. This was a loss of 679,772.

As they shed jobs, at some point between 1989 and 1991, these firms were employing 703,000; thus they were still large. That is, 1,406 multiplied by 500 equals 703,000. Thus, while these firms were large they shed 444,159 jobs. That is, 1,147,159 less 703,000 equals 444,159. Firms that became small by passing below the 500 mark shed 235,613. That is, 679,772 less 444,159 equals 235,613.

Now compare 293,013 and –235,613, and 457,009 and –444,159. Small firms added 57,400, and large firms added 12,850. This shows that boundary-crossers are almost equivalent as far as the analysis is concerned. However, even if we attribute all the boundary-crossers' gains to small firms, that does not change the argument that large businesses created all the jobs. To gain some perspective of the boundary-crossers' impact, note that in an average 2-year period, about 4 million jobs are created.

The data reported in Chapter 4 were rounded, and here, of course, they were not.

Appendix G

Census Bureau Data by Major Industry Division, 1989–91

Matrix tables for the total nonfarm economy and their major industry divisions are shown in Appendix G. These tabulations provide, for the period 1989–91, the number of firms, and employment and payrolls for both periods. These data are reproduced directly from Census Bureau floppy discs.

Table G.1
U.S. Firms, Employment, and Payrolls, by Firm Size, 1989-1991
(total private, nonfarm employment)

1989		Employment in 1991					
Employment size	Not active	0-4	5-19	20-49	50-99	100-499	500+
Not active in 1989							
Number of enterprises		974,933	192,643	39,546	13,188	8,575	978
1989 employment		0	0	0	0	0	0
1991 employment		965,324	1,695,536	1,194,911	904,356	1,605,585	1,472,136
1989 payroll ($000)		0	0	0	0	0	0
1991 payroll ($000)		31,399,172	26,824,594	21,228,933	17,743,798	33,964,597	32,342,409
0-4 Employees							
Number of enterprises	864,210	1,822,097	293,680	18,130	3,633	1,406	68
1989 employment	1,192,191	3,201,676	645,169	12,943	1,849	574	27
1991 employment	0	3,511,959	2,126,209	524,606	242,354	242,261	65,890
1989 payroll ($000)	21,999,136	66,778,507	18,764,495	2,501,245	1,092,124	1,083,219	243,413
1991 payroll ($000)	0	71,111,751	33,961,706	7,301,623	3,324,418	3,926,116	1,045,090
5-19 Employees							
Number of enterprises	252,001	229,353	940,833	64,960	2,899	585	20
1989 employment	2,246,502	1,568,128	8,776,445	938,008	35,906	7,105	253
1991 employment	0	655,199	8,813,458	1,642,111	188,176	93,262	25,978
1989 payroll ($000)	27,320,884	22,881,606	170,892,688	22,157,722	1,171,911	341,393	31,244
1991 payroll ($000)	0	14,407,896	182,211,986	32,191,350	2,806,505	1,428,587	485,057

20–49 Employees

Number of enterprises	54,070	7,909	61,552	192,395	21,361	1,685	36
1989 employment	1,631,792	224,748	1,562,620	5,862,955	829,195	61,077	1,259
1991 employment	0	15,285	880,100	5,894,736	1,308,468	249,612	28,335
1989 payroll ($000)	24,340,436	3,200,305	25,985,605	118,878,170	19,364,543	1,772,966	75,990
1991 payroll ($000)	0	863,883	18,798,833	126,723,919	26,959,854	4,338,662	657,617

50–99 Employees

Number of enterprises	17,570	1,404	3,036	19,586	53,975	9,331	49
1989 employment	1,200,503	94,016	198,141	1,196,834	3,732,374	754,320	3,610
1991 employment	0	2,398	36,682	759,040	3,752,588	1,225,276	49,456
1989 payroll ($000)	20,275,180	1,419,607	2,988,728	21,196,562	75,778,533	17,269,993	186,570
1991 payroll ($000)	0	263,887	1,116,686	16,481,913	80,873,064	25,058,452	1,150,193

100–499 Employees

Number of enterprises	11,026	574	809	1,702	8,329	45,499	1,669
1989 employment	2,062,196	96,303	139,567	256,231	1,098,396	9,098,109	622,838
1991 employment	0	927	9,262	60,896	668,646	9,266,003	1,208,350
1989 payroll ($000)	38,243,436	1,444,967	2,235,877	3,912,449	19,359,298	184,504,220	14,444,088
1991 payroll ($000)	0	177,564	345,496	1,578,954	14,647,601	200,606,156	25,979,994

500+ Employees

Number of enterprises	1,276	34	42	57	50	1,257	11,157
1989 employment	1,662,180	35,062	49,898	76,033	82,491	903,675	39,462,895
1991 employment	0	51	422	1,894	3,629	461,391	40,454,801
1989 payroll ($000)	36,137,969	731,678	918,988	1,402,563	1,801,588	16,158,121	978,653,537
1991 payroll ($000)	0	9,660	51,494	76,366	94,499	10,114,328	1,070,341,188

Source: Census Bureau's Standard Statistical Establishment List, 1989–1991, special tabulations.

Table G.2
U.S. Firms, Employment, and Payrolls, by Firm Size, 1989-1991
(agricultural services)

1989		Employment in 1991					
Employment size	Not active	0-4	5-19	20-49	50-99	100-499	500+
Not active in 1989							
Number of enterprises		22,664	3,205	306	52	31	2
1989 employment		0	0	0	0	0	0
1991 employment		18,843	26,170	8,742	(D)	(D)	(D)
1989 payroll ($000)		0	0	0	0	0	0
1991 payroll ($000)		456,315	324,629	123,656	(D)	(D)	(D)
0-4 Employees							
Number of enterprises	15,700	34,947	6,507	316	63	18	2
1989 employment	17,486	50,190	13,777	376	67	(D)	(D)
1991 employment	0	59,725	47,277	9,254	(D)	3,036	(D)
1989 payroll ($000)	265,869	909,388	313,734	31,082	9,904	(D)	(D)
1991 payroll ($000)	0	996,246	530,876	71,884	(D)	57,240	(D)
5-19 Employees							
Number of enterprises	3,073	4,052	14,421	901	46	8	0
1989 employment	25,921	28,415	129,228	12,606	508	95	0
1991 employment	0	10,665	134,824	22,624	3,036	1,396	0
1989 payroll ($000)	243,976	317,812	2,068,331	250,385	16,169	7,555	0
1991 payroll ($000)	0	220,381	2,276,718	339,541	29,766	21,014	0

20-49 Employees

Number of enterprises	362	162	698	1,431	157	15	0
1989 employment	10,439	(D)	18,024	41,592	5,905	(D)	0
1991 employment	0	309	9,545	42,418	9,695	2,263	0
1989 payroll ($000)	99,076	(D)	233,599	737,439	109,078	(D)	0
1991 payroll ($000)	0	11,149	183,549	805,340	147,921	22,342	0

50-99 Employees

Number of enterprises	74	16	45	119	239	51	0
1989 employment	(D)	(D)	2,958	7,490	15,909	4,075	0
1991 employment	0	35	484	4,351	16,290	6,661	0
1989 payroll ($000)	(D)	(D)	24,624	113,956	262,861	73,189	0
1991 payroll ($000)	0	2,112	15,478	92,967	287,390	100,195	0

100-499 Employees

Number of enterprises	33	10	8	16	52	143	2
1989 employment	5,319	(D)	1,420	2,485	6,892	26,803	(D)
1991 employment	0	(D)	111	680	(D)	27,305	(D)
1989 payroll ($000)	54,039	(D)	14,203	25,493	88,250	482,632	(D)
1991 payroll ($000)	0	(D)	3,784	12,456	(D)	547,843	(D)

500+ Employees

Number of enterprises	3	1	0	0	0	2	10
1989 employment	(D)	(D)	0	0	0	(D)	38,723
1991 employment	0	(D)	0	0	0	(D)	(D)
1989 payroll ($000)	(D)	(D)	0	0	0	(D)	843,966
1991 payroll ($000)	0	(D)	0	0	0	(D)	(D)

Source: Census Bureau's Standard Statistical Establishment List, 1989-1991, special tabulations.
(D) Deleted for purposes of confidentiality.

Table G.3
U.S. Firms, Employment, and Payrolls, by Firm Size, 1989-1991
(mining)

1989		Employment in 1991					
Employment size	Not active	0-4	5-19	20-49	50-99	100-499	500+
Not active in 1989							
Number of enterprises		4,041	989	279	72	70	15
1989 employment		0	0	0	0	0	0
1991 employment		4,196	9,316	8,301	4,932	(D)	(D)
1989 payroll ($000)		0	0	0	0	0	0
1991 payroll ($000)		223,680	213,934	225,523	141,344	(D)	(D)
0-4 Employees							
Number of enterprises	3,949	7,788	1,450	156	30	16	0
1989 employment	5,465	13,227	2,979	(D)	12	(D)	0
1991 employment	0	14,494	11,204	4,618	2,088	3,008	0
1989 payroll ($000)	147,348	328,919	119,738	(D)	16,996	(D)	0
1991 payroll ($000)	0	337,767	231,806	110,856	57,865	62,452	0
5-19 Employees							
Number of enterprises	1,287	1,042	4,093	500	31	10	0
1989 employment	12,274	7,908	39,234	6,939	414	106	0
1991 employment	0	2,792	40,542	13,285	(D)	(D)	0
1989 payroll ($000)	207,502	153,604	949,142	204,828	14,172	6,805	0
1991 payroll ($000)	0	75,710	1,004,874	317,281	(D)	(D)	0

20-49 Employees

Number of enterprises	449	97	333	1,090	186	26	0
1989 employment	13,698	(D)	8,772	32,171	7,014	(D)	0
1991 employment	0	213	4,478	33,952	11,922	3,595	0
1989 payroll ($000)	290,391	(D)	202,540	883,287	218,072	(D)	0
1991 payroll ($000)	0	9,549	128,168	951,887	318,917	92,390	0

50-99 Employees

Number of enterprises	129	13	36	110	285	86	0
1989 employment	8,812	782	2,446	6,662	19,543	6,506	0
1991 employment	0	(D)	(D)	(D)	20,008	11,231	0
1989 payroll ($000)	217,926	13,403	62,458	157,582	556,318	204,543	0
1991 payroll ($000)	0	(D)	(D)	(D)	581,433	310,161	0

100-499 Employees

Number of enterprises	79	3	8	13	29	261	16
1989 employment	14,965	(D)	1,064	2,063	4,269	52,985	(D)
1991 employment	0	(D)	(D)	(D)	(D)	56,448	(D)
1989 payroll ($000)	423,154	(D)	22,874	56,836	117,643	1,686,716	(D)
1991 payroll ($000)	0	(D)	(D)	(D)	(D)	1,875,278	(D)

500+ Employees

Number of enterprises	7	0	0	1	0	16	97
1989 employment	7,448	0	0	(D)	0	(D)	440,301
1991 employment	0	0	0	(D)	0	(D)	448,810
1989 payroll ($000)	256,030	0	0	(D)	0	(D)	16,145,934
1991 payroll ($000)	0	0	0	(D)	0	(D)	17,768,764

Source: Census Bureau's Standard Statistical Establishment List, 1989-1991, special tabulations.
(D) Deleted for purposes of confidentiality.

Table G.4
U.S. Firms, Employment, and Payrolls, by Firm Size, 1989-1991
(contract construction)

1989 Employment size	Employment in 1991						
	Not active	0-4	5-19	20-49	50-99	100-499	500+
Not active in 1989							
Number of enterprises		124,966	21,797	2,427	503	306	18
1989 employment		0	0	0	0	0	0
1991 employment		121,484	181,020	70,190	34,138	55,204	17,562
1989 payroll ($000)		0	0	0	0	0	0
1991 payroll ($000)		3,740,781	3,123,262	1,408,227	835,351	1,553,057	560,011
0-4 Employees							
Number of enterprises	121,464	209,176	37,156	2,181	332	88	4
1989 employment	163,694	350,655	75,369	2,426	247	(D)	(D)
1991 employment	0	372,284	280,083	61,499	(D)	15,219	(D)
1989 payroll ($000)	3,053,752	7,593,141	2,669,847	348,421	109,783	(D)	(D)
1991 payroll ($000)	0	7,227,005	4,614,436	933,223	(D)	267,688	(D)
5-19 Employees							
Number of enterprises	33,215	40,416	90,065	7,723	456	65	0
1989 employment	287,201	297,450	860,674	104,536	5,832	820	0
1991 employment	0	102,270	830,561	203,215	29,227	9,315	0
1989 payroll ($000)	3,930,678	4,945,535	19,867,030	3,244,525	243,379	38,994	0
1991 payroll ($000)	0	2,597,498	19,335,491	4,513,071	500,006	169,550	0

20-49 Employees

Number of enterprises	5,043	1,883	10,253	15,325	2,099	194	1
1989 employment	148,148	53,518	274,098	470,335	76,724	(D)	(D)
1991 employment	0	(D)	134,782	461,931	132,768	28,399	(D)
1989 payroll ($000)	2,439,508	861,912	6,174,769	13,368,588	2,635,405	(D)	(D)
1991 payroll ($000)	0	(D)	3,965,764	13,254,648	3,479,902	593,505	(D)

50-99 Employees

Number of enterprises	1,183	279	792	2,862	3,198	762	4
1989 employment	79,505	18,449	51,112	182,342	221,677	58,914	357
1991 employment	0	(D)	(D)	102,875	218,851	102,782	(D)
1989 payroll ($000)	1,522,915	305,022	977,031	4,784,865	6,770,634	2,122,029	19,813
1991 payroll ($000)	0	(D)	(D)	3,376,635	6,718,506	2,813,058	(D)

100-499 Employees

Number of enterprises	574	82	171	346	969	2,123	75
1989 employment	103,001	12,521	27,621	52,463	137,699	415,233	24,913
1991 employment	0	(D)	(D)	12,269	72,840	401,220	49,874
1989 payroll ($000)	2,387,237	218,067	489,829	1,130,585	3,640,932	13,532,761	948,245
1991 payroll ($000)	0	(D)	(D)	437,633	2,470,907	13,275,832	1,512,183

500+ Employees

Number of enterprises	50	3	4	4	6	91	218
1989 employment	66,121	2,168	3,721	3,571	4,138	62,593	439,113
1991 employment	0	(D)	(D)	110	(D)	30,232	(D)
1989 payroll ($000)	1,890,781	53,689	50,155	41,186	98,840	1,667,999	14,468,109
1991 payroll ($000)	0	(D)	(D)	5,165	(D)	1,077,857	(D)

Source: Census Bureau's Standard Statistical Establishment List, 1989-1991, special tabulations.
(D) Deleted for purposes of confidentiality.

Table G.5
U.S. Firms, Employment, and Payrolls, by Firm Size, 1989-1991
(manufacturing)

1989		Employment in 1991					
Employment size	Not active	0-4	5-19	20-49	50-99	100-499	500+
Not active in 1989							
Number of enterprises		45,195	13,473	3,991	1,974	1,989	222
1989 employment		0	0	0	0	0	0
1991 employment		47,010	124,506	124,084	139,086	385,893	275,902
1989 payroll ($000)		0	0	0	0	0	0
1991 payroll ($000)		2,276,588	2,221,727	2,544,410	3,179,347	9,557,415	7,493,821
0-4 Employees							
Number of enterprises	36,598	66,271	17,240	1,707	444	189	6
1989 employment	54,786	124,075	34,320	981	134	46	4
1991 employment	0	136,523	132,999	50,186	29,656	32,890	7,130
1989 payroll ($000)	1,432,215	2,469,268	1,152,775	286,560	188,971	236,503	44,813
1991 payroll ($000)	0	2,607,601	2,313,443	900,476	545,561	771,043	180,776
5-19 Employees							
Number of enterprises	18,234	14,207	73,032	6,947	297	57	0
1989 employment	173,135	102,218	747,465	102,261	3,811	717	0
1991 employment	0	40,339	734,962	175,707	19,352	10,257	0
1989 payroll ($000)	2,331,583	1,551,604	15,651,094	2,573,996	147,562	52,251	0
1991 payroll ($000)	0	900,587	16,253,273	3,802,352	363,642	178,405	0

20-49 Employees

Number of enterprises	6,396	793	8,080	28,425	3,196	214	3
1989 employment	198,515	23,269	205,799	891,959	126,150	7,773	142
1991 employment	0	1,522	118,187	879,455	193,575	31,110	1,733
1989 payroll ($000)	3,322,486	368,592	3,758,606	20,586,462	3,196,481	283,362	10,118
1991 payroll ($000)	0	103,380	2,739,863	21,578,192	4,476,042	633,713	35,162

50-99 Employees

Number of enterprises	3,175	214	435	3,797	10,530	1,610	8
1989 employment	222,286	14,616	28,484	232,256	743,080	131,973	525
1991 employment	0	336	5,492	149,510	731,058	205,614	8,090
1989 payroll ($000)	4,246,496	249,316	473,553	4,515,572	17,402,164	3,464,104	62,966
1991 payroll ($000)	0	36,234	181,447	3,574,229	18,231,434	4,983,268	227,867

100-499 Employees

Number of enterprises	2,814	101	148	280	1,976	10,374	308
1989 employment	551,146	16,677	26,311	42,357	255,184	2,179,756	119,435
1991 employment	0	167	1,609	10,353	159,720	2,123,294	216,712
1989 payroll ($000)	11,532,324	334,478	491,138	715,651	5,067,723	50,640,240	3,295,757
1991 payroll ($000)	0	19,481	60,003	304,548	3,840,982	53,036,740	5,788,400

500+ Employees

Number of enterprises	313	4	10	8	6	408	3,061
1989 employment	420,712	3,616	9,482	9,415	4,707	269,374	13,046,483
1991 employment	0	7	106	233	419	155,380	12,601,491
1989 payroll ($000)	10,888,877	82,098	169,947	193,046	87,715	5,752,720	406,961,566
1991 payroll ($000)	0	313	4,189	8,628	9,430	3,800,138	420,524,001

Source: Census Bureau's Standard Statistical Establishment List, 1989-1991, special tabulations.

Table G.6
U.S. Firms, Employment, and Payrolls, by Firm Size, 1989-1991
(transportation, communication, and public utilities)

1989 Employment size	Not active	Employment in 1991					
		0-4	5-19	20-49	50-99	100-499	500+
Not active in 1989							
Number of enterprises		39,550	7,753	2,061	783	539	63
1989 employment		0	0	0	0	0	0
1991 employment		38,856	69,646	62,319	(D)	100,138	(D)
1989 payroll ($000)		0	0	0	0	0	0
1991 payroll ($000)		1,308,798	1,183,259	1,237,506	(D)	2,438,548	(D)
0-4 Employees							
Number of enterprises	33,193	57,596	10,548	813	(D)	61	3
1989 employment	45,784	98,081	21,998	(D)	(D)	(D)	(D)
1991 employment	0	110,499	78,748	23,198	(D)	9,873	(D)
1989 payroll ($000)	874,572	1,834,576	650,836	(D)	(D)	(D)	(D)
1991 payroll ($000)	0	1,946,863	1,252,230	374,863	(D)	200,977	(D)
5-19 Employees							
Number of enterprises	10,429	7,801	31,139	2,832	138	38	1
1989 employment	97,652	54,929	297,164	40,478	(D)	(D)	(D)
1991 employment	0	21,632	301,180	72,913	(D)	6,228	(D)
1989 payroll ($000)	1,380,543	775,294	5,599,655	920,307	(D)	(D)	(D)
1991 payroll ($000)	0	456,391	5,938,341	1,383,638	(D)	104,604	(D)

20-49 Employees

Number of enterprises	2,856	365	2,387	7,825	963	83	3
1989 employment	86,345	10,435	60,737	236,412	36,881	3,086	95
1991 employment	0	681	34,059	241,474	59,267	12,237	3,044
1989 payroll ($000)	1,494,456	159,486	1,025,754	5,039,548	924,015	87,586	5,168
1991 payroll ($000)	0	37,038	736,946	5,379,273	1,264,194	246,387	49,491

50-99 Employees

Number of enterprises	1,025	86	120	682	2,172	375	3
1989 employment	(D)	(D)	(D)	41,591	147,649	30,067	(D)
1991 employment	0	(D)	(D)	(D)	151,638	50,342	(D)
1989 payroll ($000)	(D)	(D)	(D)	764,548	3,344,224	727,301	(D)
1991 payroll ($000)	0	(D)	(D)	(D)	3,624,250	1,074,097	(D)

100-499 Employees

Number of enterprises	670	38	36	65	232	1,672	79
1989 employment	126,971	6,229	5,769	9,530	29,882	326,494	29,126
1991 employment	0	(D)	428	(D)	19,011	344,772	58,319
1989 payroll ($000)	2,640,690	99,273	90,121	148,272	567,416	8,015,733	794,376
1991 payroll ($000)	0	(D)	25,837	(D)	440,685	8,851,233	1,382,635

500+ Employees

Number of enterprises	80	3	3	1	3	31	545
1989 employment	(D)	(D)	(D)	(D)	(D)	22,050	3,452,521
1991 employment	0	(D)	(D)	(D)	(D)	11,743	3,653,395
1989 payroll ($000)	(D)	(D)	(D)	(D)	(D)	428,994	114,487,267
1991 payroll ($000)	0	(D)	(D)	(D)	(D)	284,964	129,578,248

Source: Census Bureau's Standard Statistical Establishment List, 1989-1991, special tabulations.
(D) Deleted for purposes of confidentiality.

Table G.7
U.S. Firms, Employment, and Payrolls, by Firm Size, 1989-1991
(wholesale trade)

1989		Employment in 1991						
Employment size	Not active	0-4	5-19	20-49	50-99	100-499	500+	
Not active in 1989								
Number of enterprises		60,075	12,222	2,355	799	398	33	
1989 employment		0	0	0	0	0	0	
1991 employment		64,104	106,130	71,835	54,322	71,458	37,191	
1989 payroll ($000)		0	0	0	0	0	0	
1991 payroll ($000)		2,410,839	2,331,868	1,762,082	1,373,981	1,762,855	1,182,071	
0-4 Employees								
Number of enterprises	49,366	112,394	20,672	985	151	60	2	
1989 employment	74,566	207,015	48,661	(D)	(D)	(D)	(D)	
1991 employment	0	225,871	147,115	27,657	(D)	9,758	(D)	
1989 payroll ($000)	1,620,149	5,760,680	1,769,988	(D)	(D)	(D)	(D)	
1991 payroll ($000)	0	6,055,266	3,263,763	536,679	(D)	214,494	(D)	
5-19 Employees								
Number of enterprises	17,635	16,158	89,303	6,503	244	44	0	
1989 employment	160,352	109,551	861,876	96,387	2,988	585	0	
1991 employment	0	47,540	872,713	161,319	15,853	6,646	0	
1989 payroll ($000)	2,692,213	2,029,027	21,437,187	2,825,920	103,972	34,152	0	
1991 payroll ($000)	0	1,264,390	22,736,368	4,048,899	268,905	142,354	0	

20-49 Employees

Number of enterprises	4,059	601	5,497	22,015	2,213	135	2
1989 employment	123,612	17,330	135,791	664,955	87,599	(D)	(D)
1991 employment	0	(D)	81,851	673,564	134,262	19,139	(D)
1989 payroll ($000)	2,530,372	308,675	2,853,869	17,073,652	2,514,471	(D)	(D)
1991 payroll ($000)	0	(D).	2,159,582	18,085,027	3,470,297	426,875	(D)

50-99 Employees

Number of enterprises	1,283	99	222	1,635	5,462	836	7
1989 employment	87,060	(D)	(D)	97,141	374,547	69,009	(D)
1991 employment	0	183	2,620	65,381	380,585	106,769	5,290
1989 payroll ($000)	1,933,958	(D)	(D)	2,165,874	9,705,813	1,909,459	(D)
1991 payroll ($000)	0	19,378	82,551	1,764,069	10,282,311	2,740,741	161,470

100-499 Employees

Number of enterprises	681	45	56	130	627	3,648	111
1989 employment	121,967	7,405	8,916	18,531	80,932	693,968	39,292
1991 employment	0	(D)	(D)	(D)	(D)	716,934	76,995
1989 payroll ($000)	2,754,278	133,770	162,749	350,294	1,800,527	18,229,773	1,168,042
1991 payroll ($000)	0	(D)	(D)	(D)	(D)	19,852,027	2,142,281

500+ Employees

Number of enterprises	44	1	1	2	2	63	477
1989 employment	42,232	(D)	(D)	(D)	(D)	41,395	1,060,192
1991 employment	0	(D)	(D)	(D)	(D)	23,365	1,135,805
1989 payroll ($000)	1,133,492	(D)	(D)	(D)	(D)	980,306	30,849,017
1991 payroll ($000)	0	(D)	(D)	(D)	(D)	643,580	35,173,495

Source: Census Bureau's Standard Statistical Establishment List, 1989-1991, special tabulations.
(D) Deleted for purposes of confidentiality.

Table G.8
U.S. Firms, Employment, and Payrolls, by Firm Size, 1989-1991
(retail trade)

1989 Employment size	Not active	Employment in 1991					
		0-4	5-19	20-49	50-99	100-499	500+
Not active in 1989							
Number of enterprises		214,045	55,408	11,653	3,165	1,196	83
1989 employment		0	0	0	0	0	0
1991 employment		215,000	499,825	349,196	211,698	210,919	179,538
1989 payroll ($000)		0	0	0	0	0	0
1991 payroll ($000)		4,848,165	4,466,671	3,458,347	2,331,223	2,381,815	2,518,267
0-4 Employees							
Number of enterprises	196,584	339,975	66,980	5,441	1,008	174	4
1989 employment	301,951	627,214	133,571	2,013	(D)	72	(D)
1991 employment	0	698,087	495,988	158,725	(D)	(D)	2,370
1989 payroll ($000)	3,147,434	7,538,521	2,560,617	557,161	(D)	98,872	(D)
1991 payroll ($000)	0	7,999,979	4,577,493	1,460,245	(D)	(D)	25,378
5-19 Employees							
Number of enterprises	75,965	51,670	228,259	13,577	416	64	1
1989 employment	679,456	347,686	2,176,979	199,361	(D)	(D)	(D)
1991 employment	0	153,240	2,145,655	337,924	(D)	(D)	(D)
1989 payroll ($000)	4,754,467	3,063,499	25,202,531	2,571,190	(D)	(D)	(D)
1991 payroll ($000)	0	1,982,062	26,050,449	3,544,900	(D)	(D)	(D)

20-49 Employees

Number of enterprises	15,297	1,471	16,049	49,265	4,227	236	3
1989 employment	455,465	41,299	400,623	1,525,543	166,338	(D)	(D)
1991 employment	0	2,535	234,765	1,493,442	256,177	33,500	2,648
1989 payroll ($000)	3,854,503	368,110	3,942,505	19,404,592	2,312,909	(D)	(D)
1991 payroll ($000)	0	96,678	2,950,904	19,792,182	3,035,789	345,971	20,935

50-99 Employees

Number of enterprises	4,048	234	479	5,252	12,767	1,496	4
1989 employment	271,530	(D)	30,833	315,975	882,354	120,893	(D)
1991 employment	0	(D)	5,734	207,565	863,974	195,981	(D)
1989 payroll ($000)	2,778,140	(D)	266,372	3,588,927	12,858,974	1,691,763	(D)
1991 payroll ($000)	0	(D)	92,610	2,861,389	13,089,060	2,407,529	(D)

100-499 Employees

Number of enterprises	1,463	77	95	282	1,862	7,539	239
1989 employment	253,931	13,009	16,201	40,587	239,273	1,469,842	89,676
1991 employment	0	120	1,117	10,017	150,753	1,473,324	163,639
1989 payroll ($000)	2,789,826	111,920	165,017	346,519	2,873,605	19,148,991	1,1`3,515
1991 payroll ($000)	0	12,624	20,290	129,226	2,269,351	20,382,969	1,921,547

500+ Employees

Number of enterprises	113	2	7	14	5	186	1,500
1989 employment	147,011	(D)	7,371	28,213	(D)	146,281	8,301,015
1991 employment	0	(D)	67	445	(D)	68,778	8,550,638
1989 payroll ($000)	1,555,530	(D)	89,712	398,731	(D)	1,510,385	104,764,957
1991 payroll ($000)	0	(D)	2,467	6,503	(D)	854,790	115,916,360

Source: Census Bureau's Standard Statistical Establishment List, 1989-1991, special tabulations.
(D) Deleted for purposes of confidentiality.

Table G.9
U.S. Firms, Employment, and Payrolls, by Firm Size, 1989-1991
(finance, insurance, and real estate)

1989		Employment in 1991					
Employment size	Not active	0-4	5-19	20-49	50-99	100-499	500+
Not active in 1989							
Number of enterprises		84,650	13,398	6,177	2,479	1,419	117
1989 employment		0	0	0	0	0	0
1991 employment		77,940	130,159	191,927	169,131	257,723	156,361
1989 payroll ($000)		0	0	0	0	0	0
1991 payroll ($000)		3,187,836	3,102,572	4,792,348	4,365,512	6,914,515	4,729,975
0-4 Employees							
Number of enterprises	76,208	198,964	17,059	804	163	79	6
1989 employment	98,542	329,055	40,596	(D)	101	(D)	(D)
1991 employment	0	354,129	117,474	23,186	10,823	(D)	(D)
1989 payroll ($000)	2,630,381	6,641,231	1,291,993	(D)	56,333	(D)	(D)
1991 payroll ($000)	0	6,899,769	2,332,726	415,857	198,526	(D)	(D)
5-19 Employees							
Number of enterprises	17,637	13,824	50,930	2,575	131	32	4
1989 employment	170,113	91,615	450,638	36,665	1,571	(D)	(D)
1991 employment	0	40,012	453,473	65,205	8,751	(D)	(D)
1989 payroll ($000)	3,610,497	1,670,391	10,733,669	1,072,193	62,223	(D)	(D)
1991 payroll ($000)	0	1,014,213	11,354,862	1,593,313	174,648	(D)	(D)

20-49 Employees

Number of enterprises	7,307	431	2,214	7,665	769	77	9
1989 employment	226,466	12,132	56,394	229,328	30,131	2,671	269
1991 employment	0	838	31,086	234,348	46,793	12,130	7,709
1989 payroll ($000)	5,125,473	198,947	1,260,531	5,674,716	876,864	100,268	15,717
1991 payroll ($000)	0	55,612	825,979	6,110,453	1,232,674	290,928	262,657

50-99 Employees

Number of enterprises	2,704	80	158	623	2,036	369	4
1989 employment	185,060	(D)	(D)	37,916	139,953	30,107	(D)
1991 employment	0	113	1,811	23,915	142,586	49,185	5,862
1989 payroll ($000)	4,127,467	(D)	(D)	846,309	3,384,654	908,309	(D)
1991 payroll ($000)	0	17,687	62,123	616,894	3,639,923	1,363,767	153,071

100-499 Employees

Number of enterprises	1,515	45	55	57	287	2,244	110
1989 employment	268,231	7,978	10,956	9,434	37,154	463,492	42,638
1991 employment	0	(D)	(D)	(D)	23,499	473,730	71,825
1989 payroll ($000)	6,336,167	135,782	245,138	188,281	824,670	11,387,120	1,159,788
1991 payroll ($000)	0	(D)	(D)	(D)	597,716	12,275,214	2,011,971

500+ Employees

Number of enterprises	158	8	3	3	8	78	901
1989 employment	175,751	(D)	(D)	(D)	22,315	85,958	3,433,928
1991 employment	0	(D)	(D)	(D)	595	26,034	3,657,121
1989 payroll ($000)	4,693,858	(D)	(D)	(D)	594,343	2,015,370	101,298,533
1991 payroll ($000)	0	(D)	(D)	(D)	19,106	720,935	114,538,844

Source: Census Bureau's Standard Statistical Establishment List, 1989-1991, special tabulations.
(D) Deleted for purposes of confidentiality.

Table G.10
U.S. Firms, Employment, and Payrolls, by Firm Size, 1989-1991
(services)

1989 Employment size	Employment in 1991						
	Not active	0-4	5-19	20-49	50-99	100-499	500+
Not active in 1989							
Number of enterprises		356,964	62,691	10,076	3,361	2,627	425
1989 employment		0	0	0	0	0	0
1991 employment		363,994	534,060	301,435	233,035	505,268	710,351
1989 payroll ($000)		0	0	0	0	0	0
1991 payroll ($000)		12,626,751	9,767,474	5,628,678	4,274,742	8,808,033	13,297,036
0-4 Employees							
Number of enterprises	274,798	791,417	115,754	5,694	1,308	721	41
1989 employment	390,869	1,399,425	273,606	4,604	786	(D)	(D)
1991 employment	0	1,536,063	812,816	165,263	88,976	126,892	42,540
1989 payroll ($000)	7,414,718	33,657,090	8,223,863	806,316	382,728	(D)	(D)
1991 payroll ($000)	0	36,992,480	14,825,082	2,487,362	1,182,073	1,724,153	578,632
5-19 Employees							
Number of enterprises	69,110	80,050	359,421	23,387	1,140	267	14
1989 employment	594,612	527,379	3,211,734	338,609	13,963	(D)	(D)
1991 employment	0	236,451	3,297,998	589,559	73,875	43,228	17,117
1989 payroll ($000)	7,874,237	8,366,599	69,369,051	8,491,108	433,938	(D)	(D)
1991 payroll ($000)	0	5,892,968	77,247,041	12,641,933	1,076,309	574,400	241,671

20-49 Employees

Number of enterprises	11,447	2,093	16,024	59,333	7,551	705	15
1989 employment	343,096	59,150	401,874	1,769,971	292,453	25,509	515
1991 employment	0	4,079	231,116	1,833,441	464,009	107,239	11,402
1989 payroll ($000)	4,992,241	846,306	6,528,280	36,102,251	6,577,248	652,031	32,739
1991 payroll ($000)	0	281,095	5,105,561	40,759,006	9,534,118	1,686,551	252,079

50-99 Employees

Number of enterprises	3,834	383	749	4,506	17,286	3,746	19
1989 employment	262,554	25,926	49,527	275,461	1,187,662	302,776	1,404
1991 employment	0	682	9,023	174,592	1,227,598	496,711	22,587
1989 payroll ($000)	3,957,944	347,086	617,081	4,258,929	21,492,891	6,169,296	35,110
1991 payroll ($000)	0	90,017	274,703	3,473,689	24,418,757	9,265,636	448,315

100-499 Employees

Number of enterprises	3,115	173	232	513	2,295	17,495	729
1989 employment	600,167	30,640	41,309	78,781	307,111	3,469,536	270,433
1991 employment	0	(D)	(D)	18,311	184,938	3,648,976	559,288
1989 payroll ($000)	9,109,259	396,741	554,808	950,518	4,378,532	61,380,254	5,661,762
1991 payroll ($000)	0	(D)	(D)	436,204	3,523,478	70,509,020	10,843,006

500+ Employees

Number of enterprises	494	12	14	24	20	382	4,348
1989 employment	664,008	11,224	19,393	24,288	38,706	263,233	9,250,619
1991 employment	0	(D)	(D)	833	1,386	138,783	9,895,427
1989 payroll ($000)	12,354,535	213,207	328,503	513,755	770,182	3,439,707	188,834,188
1991 payroll ($000)	0	(D)	(D)	45,519	34,949	2,516,053	219,747,546

Source: Census Bureau's Standard Statistical Establishment List, 1989-1991, special tabulations.
(D) Deleted for purposes of confidentiality.

Table G.11
U.S. Firms, Employment, and Payrolls, by Firm Size, 1989-1991
(unclassified)

1989 Employment size		Employment in 1991					
	Not active	0-4	5-19	20-49	50-99	100-499	500+
Not active in 1989							
Number of enterprises		22,783	1,707	221	0	0	0
1989 employment		0	0	0	0	0	0
1991 employment		13,897	14,704	6,882	0	0	0
1989 payroll ($000)		0	0	0	0	0	0
1991 payroll ($000)		319,419	89,198	48,156	0	0	0
0-4 Employees							
Number of enterprises	56,350	3,569	314	33	0	0	0
1989 employment	39,048	2,739	292	11	0	0	0
1991 employment	0	4,284	2,505	1,020	0	0	0
1989 payroll ($000)	1,412,698	45,693	11,104	3,326	0	0	0
1991 payroll ($000)	0	48,775	19,851	10,178	0	0	0
5-19 Employees							
Number of enterprises	5,416	133	170	15	0	0	0
1989 employment	45,786	977	1,453	166	0	0	0
1991 employment	0	258	1,550	360	0	0	0
1989 payroll ($000)	295,188	8,241	14,998	3,270	0	0	0
1991 payroll ($000)	0	3,696	14,569	6,422	0	0	0

20-49 Employees

Number of enterprises	854	13	17	21	0	0	0	0	0	0	0	0	0	0	0	0
1989 employment	26,008	324	508	689	0	0	0	0	0	0	0	0	0	0	0	0
1991 employment	0	18	231	711	0	0	0	0	0	0	0	0	0	0	0	0
1989 payroll ($000)	191,930	1,556	5,152	7,635	0	0	0	0	0	0	0	0	0	0	0	0
1991 payroll ($000)	0	705	2,517	7,911	0	0	0	0	0	0	0	0	0	0	0	0

50-99 Employees

Number of enterprises	115	0	0	0	0	0	0	0	0	0	0	0	0	0	0	0
1989 employment	7,836	0	0	0	0	0	0	0	0	0	0	0	0	0	0	0
1991 employment	0	0	0	0	0	0	0	0	0	0	0	0	0	0	0	0
1989 payroll ($000)	64,812	0	0	0	0	0	0	0	0	0	0	0	0	0	0	0
1991 payroll ($000)	0	0	0	0	0	0	0	0	0	0	0	0	0	0	0	0

100-499 Employees

Number of enterprises	82	0	0	0	0	0	0	0	0	0	0	0	0	0	0	0
1989 employment	16,498	0	0	0	0	0	0	0	0	0	0	0	0	0	0	0
1991 employment	0	0	0	0	0	0	0	0	0	0	0	0	0	0	0	0
1989 payroll ($000)	216,462	0	0	0	0	0	0	0	0	0	0	0	0	0	0	0
1991 payroll ($000)	0	0	0	0	0	0	0	0	0	0	0	0	0	0	0	0

500+ Employees

Number of enterprises	14	0	0	0	0	0	0	0	0	0	0	0	0	0	0	0
1989 employment	11,121	0	0	0	0	0	0	0	0	0	0	0	0	0	0	0
1991 employment	0	0	0	0	0	0	0	0	0	0	0	0	0	0	0	0
1989 payroll ($000)	179,321	0	0	0	0	0	0	0	0	0	0	0	0	0	0	0
1991 payroll ($000)	0	0	0	0	0	0	0	0	0	0	0	0	0	0	0	0

Source: Census Bureau's Standard Statistical Establishment List, 1989-1991, special tabulations.

Bibliography

Baldwin, John, and Garnett Picot. (1994). "Employment Generated by Small Producers in the Canadian Manufacturing Sector." *Statistics Canada.*

Birch, David. (1979). "The Job Generation Process." A report to the U.S. Department of Commerce, Economic Development Administration.

Brown, Charles, James Hamilton, and James Medoff. (1990). "Employers Large and Small." Cambridge, MA: Harvard University Press.

Bureau of the Census. (1990). "1989 Statistical Abstract of the United States." Washington, DC: U.S. Government Printing Office.

Bureau of the Census. (1979). "The Standard Statistical Establishment List." Technical Paper 44.

Davis, Steven J.; John Haltiwanger; and Scott Schuh. *Small Business and Job Creation: Dissecting the Myth and Reassessing the Facts.* NBER Working Paper #4492. New York: National Bureau of Economic Research, 1993.

Dennis, William, Jr., Bruce Phillips, Edward Starr. (1994). "Small Business Job Creation, The Findings and their Critics." *Business Economics* (July).

Dentzer, Susan. (1993). "Doing the Small Business Shuffle." *U.S. News and World Report* (August 16), p. 49.

Epstein, Gene. (1994). "The Real Engine of U.S. Employment Growth Might Be Bigger Than Many Believe." *Barron's* (May 23) 29:1.

Friedman, Milton. (1992). "Do Old Fallacies Ever Die?" *Journal of Economic Literature*, (December 30), no. 4, pp. 2129–32.

Gibrat, R. (1930). "Les Inegalites Economiques." Paris.

Jackson, John E. "Firm Size Dynamics in a Market Economy." Paper prepared for the research group of the White House Conference on Small Business, University of Michigan, September 1994.

154

Leonard, Jonathan. (1986). "On the Size Distribution of Employment and Establishments. NBER Working Paper #1951. New York: National Bureau of Economic Research, 1986.

Lewis, Charles. (1994). "In Sickness and in Wealth: How a Swarm of Lobbyists Cornered the Debate on Health Care." *The Washington Post* (August 1), C2.

Kendall, M.G. (1948). "The Advanced Theory of Statistics," vol. 1., p. 327. London: Charles Griffin.

Hirschberg, David. (1996). "Small-Biz Blarney: What does It Take to Kill a Bad Number?" *SLATE* (online magazine, www.slate.com).

Hirschberg, David. (1994). "On the Formation of Business Firms." *Monthly Labor Review* (October).

Picot, G., J. Baldwin, and R. Dupuy. "Have Small Businesses Created a Disproportionate Share of New Jobs in Canada?" *Statistics Canada* (June 1994).

Shao, Maria. (1993). "A Question of Size: Economists Poke Holes in Notion That Little Companies Are Big Engines of Job Growth." *Boston Globe* (June 25), p. 1, Business Section.

Simon, Herbert, and Charles Bonini. (1958). "The Size Distribution of Business Firms." *American Economic Review*, (September), pp. 607–617.

Small Business Administration, Office of Advocacy. (1994). Press Release. "New Data Show Smallest Firms A Nation's Greatest Job Creators." (September 30). Washington, DC: U.S. Government Printing Office.

Small Business Administration, Office of Advocacy. (1994). "The White House Conference on Small Business." (April). Washington, DC: U.S. Government Printing Office.

Small Business Administration, Office of Advocacy. (1994). "Small Business Job-Generation: From Revolutionary Idea To Proven Fact." "The Small Business Advocate." (September). Washington, DC: U.S. Government Printing Office.

Small Business Administration, Office of Advocacy. (1994). Memo from Hirschberg to Administrator: "Job-Generation Data Problems—What the New Administrator Should Be Told." (May 3). Washington, DC: U.S. Government Printing Office.

Small Business Administration, Office of Advocacy. (1992). Business Answer Card.

Small Business Administration, Office of Advocacy. (1991). "The State of Small Business: A Report of the President. Washington, DC: U.S. Government Printing Office.

BIBLIOGRAPHY

Small Business Administration, Office of the Inspector General. (1991). Audit Report No. 1-4-001-277 (July).

Small Business Administration, Office of Advocacy. (1988). "The Hyping of Small-Firm Job Employees." *Wall Street Journal* (November 8), section 2, p. 1, column 3.

Wessel, David, and Buck Brown. (1988). "The Hyping of Small-Firm Job Employees." *Wall Street Journal* (November 8), section 2, p.1, column 3.

Wiatrowski, William. (1994). "Small Businesses and Their Employees." *Monthly Labor Review.*

Index

About the Author

David Hirschberg is a consultant in the Washington area. He has over 40 years experience as a U.S. government economist/statician. He has been employed by several U.S. government statistical agencies, including the Department of Commerce, Bureau of Economic Analysis; the Department of Labor, Bureau of Labor Statistics; and the Social Security Administration, Office of Economic Research. From 1979 until his retirement in 1995, he worked for the Small Business Administration, Office of Advocacy.